The Avoidant Attachment Handbook

Overcome Fear of Intimacy, Discover the Triggers of Deactivation and Move to a Safe Attachment Style

Giuli Sharon

©Copyright - All rights reserved.

Copyright:

The content contained within this book may not be reproduced, duplicated, or transmitted without direct written permission from the author or publisher.

Under no circumstances will any blame or legal responsibility be held against the publisher or author for any damages, reparation, or monetary loss due to the information contained within this book, either directly or indirectly.

Legal Notice:

This book is copyright protected and is intended for personal use only. No part of this book may be amended, distributed, sold, quoted, or paraphrased without the consent of the author or publisher.

Disclaimer Notice:

The information in this book is provided for educational and entertainment purposes only. Every effort has been made to ensure the accuracy and reliability of the information. However, no warranties of any kind, expressed or implied, are made. Readers acknowledge that the author is not providing legal, financial, medical, or professional advice.

The content has been compiled from various sources. It is advised to consult a licensed professional before attempting any techniques described in this book.

By reading this book, the reader agrees that the author shall not be held responsible.

Staten House

ISBN: 979-8-89965-139-7

Index

Introduction 6

Chapter 1: Understanding Attachment 9
   1.1 The History of Avoidant Attachment 10
   1.2 Profile of an Avoidant: Characteristics and Behaviours 11
   1.3 Differences From Other Attachment Styles 13

Chapter 2: Real Life Stories 16
   2.1 Experiences and Testimonies: Personal Accounts of Those Who Have Experienced Avoidant Attachment 18
   2.2 Overcoming Loneliness and Rejection 20
   2.3 Transformation and Healing 23

Chapter 3: The Science of Attachment 26
   3.1 Neuroscientific Foundations of Attachment 27
   3.2 The Influence of Childhood on Adult Attachment Style 29
   3.3 Recent Studies and Research 32

Chapter 4: Custom Emotional Maps 35
   4.1 Creating Your Own Emotional Map 37
   4.2 Identifying Patterns and Triggers 39
   4.3 Using the Personal Growth Map 41

Chapter 5: Mindfulness and Presence Techniques 44
   5.1 Fundamentals of Mindfulness 46
   5.2 Practical Exercises to Raise Awareness 49
   5.3 Applications in Daily Life 52

Chapter 6: Conscious Communication 55
  6.1 Principles of Effective Communication 57
  6.2 Overcoming Barriers to Vulnerability 59
  6.3 Tools to Improve Connection 62

Chapter 7: Rebuilding Trust 65
  7.1 Facing and Overcoming the Wounds of the Past 67
  7.2 Steps to Self-Confidence and Others: Building Confidence in Self and Others 69
  7.3 Reconnecting with Intimacy 72

Chapter 8: From Theory to Practice 74
  8.1 Daily Strategies for Change 77
  8.2 Setting Goals and Tracking Progress 81
  8.3 Maintaining Change Over Time 84

Chapter 9: Personal Action Plan 87
  9.1 Developing Your Action Plan 89
  9.2 Setting Short-Term and Long-Term Goals 91
  9.3 Resources and Tools for Success 94

Chapter 10: Towards a Future of Growth and Sustainability 96
  10.1 Finding and Cultivating Purpose in Life 98
  10.2 Sustainable Personal Energy Management 101
  10.3 Continuous Commitment to Learning and Adaptation 104

Conclusion 106

BONUS 108

Introduction

Interpersonal relationships are at the heart of our human experience. We want them to prevent us from realizing deep and satisfying relationships. In the modern era, the challenges of relationships are many: from technological overload to the speed of daily life, to cultural changes that affect relationship dynamics. These difficulties can be amplified by more personal issues, such as our fears, insecurities, and attachment styles. Avoidant attachment is one of the most common and least understood obstacles that people face in their relationships. People with avoidant attachment tend to avoid intimacy and withdraw emotionally, often without realizing it. This can lead to a relationship life characterized by emotional isolation, misunderstandings, and dissatisfaction. Understanding and overcoming avoidant attachment is essential for anyone looking to build healthier and more satisfying relationships.

Why This Book Is Different

Unlike many other books on relationships, "Safe Relationships" doesn't offer superficial or quick fixes. This book is a practical and comprehensive guide that combines theory, real-world examples, and practical tools to help you transform your relationship life. Each chapter includes practical exercises that will guide you step by step through the process of personal and relational growth.

In addition to explaining attachment theories in a clear and accessible way, this book will provide you with concrete exercises to do. These exercises are designed to help you reflect on your experiences, identify your attachment patterns, and develop new interpersonal skills.

To make the concepts more tangible, each chapter includes real-world stories and examples. These tales illustrate how the theories and strategies presented can be applied in everyday life, showing the successes and challenges of real people.

We've included citations and references to scientific studies to ensure the credibility of the content, providing a solid foundation on which to build your understanding of relationship dynamics. Each concept presented is supported by research in the fields of psychology and social sciences.

How to use this book

This book is structured to be read sequentially, but you can also choose to focus on the chapters that you feel are most relevant to your current situation. Each chapter includes practical exercises that we encourage you to complete to apply what you've learned to your daily life.

We recommend that you take your time and reflect on the questions and exercises. Real change takes time and effort, so don't rush. Every step forward is a major milestone.

Keep a journal of your reflections and progress as you work through the book. Writing down your thoughts and experiences can help you track your growth path and see improvements over time. This journal will become a valuable travel companion, providing you with a clear picture of your progress.

Although the book is designed to be read in order, you can skip back and forth between chapters as per your requirement. For example, if you are currently facing conflict in a relationship, you may want to read the chapter on conflict management first.

A Path of Personal and Relational Growth

Deep and meaningful relationships are crucial to our emotional and psychological well-being. However, building such relationships requires commitment, introspection, and a willingness to face your fears and insecurities. This book will guide you on a journey of self-discovery, helping you better understand yourself and develop the skills you need to improve your relationships.

Changing one's attachment patterns is not an easy process, but it is extremely rewarding. It requires commitment and perseverance, but the benefits that come with it, such as more satisfying relationships and greater emotional stability, are worth every effort.

In addition to the content of the book, we encourage you to seek support from a therapist or support group if needed. Having a professional by your side can accelerate your growth path and provide additional clarity and support.

Start Your Journey

If you are ready to embark on this path of personal and relational growth, take this book as your travel companion. Each chapter has been carefully designed to give you the knowledge and tools you need to transform your relationship life. Take the time to absorb the information, do the exercises, and reflect on your experiences. The journey to safe and satisfying relationships is an ongoing process, and every step forward is a significant milestone.

Let's start this journey of discovery and growth together. The relationships you want are within your reach – all you need is the courage to face your fears and the determination to improve.

Chapter 1: Understanding Attachment

Avoidant attachment is a behaviour that can profoundly affect our relationships and emotional life. This attachment style, first studied by John Bowlby and Mary Ainsworth, often develops in response to a childhood characterized by emotionally cold or incoherent role models. Children who grow up in these environments learn to suppress their needs for closeness and rely only on themselves to avoid the pain of rejection and disappointment. In adulthood, this strategy of self-sufficiency manifests itself through behaviours of emotional detachment and avoidance of intimacy. People with avoidant attachment may appear independent and self-sufficient, but behind this façade lies a deep fear of being hurt. These individuals tend to downplay the importance of emotional relationships, focusing on practical and logical aspects of life. However, this advocacy can lead to a sense of isolation and the difficulty of creating deep and meaningful bonds. Understanding avoidant attachment means recognizing how past experiences affect our current behaviour's. It is a journey of inner discovery that requires courage and openness. Often, these behaviours are unconscious and rooted in early life experiences. Understanding the roots of these dynamics allows us to start working on ourselves, developing greater awareness and the ability to change. The first step in overcoming avoidant attachment is to recognize it. This involves a deep reflection on one's own patterns of behaviors and the fears that fuel them. It's helpful to explore the origins of these behavior's and how they've been helpful in surviving difficult situations in the past. However, what was once a survival strategy can now be an obstacle to an emotionally satisfying life.

Once demand patterns have been reconstituted, it is possible to begin work on them through the practice of mindfulness and emotional awareness. These techniques help us live in the present, recognize our feelings, and respond in a healthier, more conscious way. Additionally, working on our relationships, learning to communicate more openly and vulnerably, can help build deeper and more meaningful bonds. Avoidant attachment is not an immutable destiny. With commitment and awareness, it is possible to transform these patterns and create a life richer in authentic and fulfilling connections. This chapter lays the foundation for our growth journey, offering a deep understanding of what it means to live with an avoidant attachment and how to begin to change. As you read on, you'll discover real-life stories, practical tools, and techniques that will help you overcome these difficulties. Get ready to explore the depths of your emotions and embark on a journey of personal transformation. Understanding is only the first step, but it is a critical step towards a more authentic and connected life. Are you ready to start this journey of discovery and change? Let's move forward together.

1.1 The History of Avoidant Attachment

Avoidant attachment, as a concept, has its roots in the theories of British psychiatrist John Bowlby, developed in the mid-twentieth century. Bowlby observed how children develop emotional bonds with their caregivers and how these early experiences affect future relationships. Through detailed observations and longitudinal studies, Bowlby found that children who received unconscious or inconsistent care often developed self-reliance strategies to cope with a lack of emotional support.

Mary Ainsworth, Bowlby's collaborator, contributed significantly to these discoveries with her experiment known as the "Strange Situation". Through this experiment, Ainsworth identified different attachment styles in children: secure, anxious-ambivalent, and avoidant. Children with avoidant attachment tended to ignore the mother figure after a period of separation, showing a kind of indifference. This behaviour was interpreted as a defence mechanism against anxiety stemming from an inconsistent attachment figure.

In the years since, research on avoidant attachment has expanded, including studies of brain development and evolutionary psychology. It found that children with avoidant attachment often grow up in environments where their emotional needs are not adequately met, leading them to develop early emotional autonomy. This attachment Style becomes a model for future relationships, influencing how individuals connect with others and manage intimacy.

Understanding the history of avoidant attachment is critical to recognizing how these early experiences shape adult behaviours. This is not only an interesting psychological theory, but a lens through which we can see and interpret our emotional and relational reactions. This historical context helps us understand the deep roots of avoidant attachment, offering a foundation for change and personal growth.

Through awareness of how avoidant attachment develops, we can begin to explore ways to transform these patterns of behavior. History teaches us that, even if these dynamics are deeply rooted in our psyche, with commitment and introspection it is possible to create new, healthier and more fulfilling ways of relating.

1.2 Profile of an Avoidant: Characteristics and Behaviours

Individuals with an avoidant attachment develop several distinctive characteristics and behaviour's, often stemming from their early life experiences. These traits, rooted in emotional survival strategies, profoundly affect how they relate to others. Below we look at the main characteristics and behaviour's that define an avoidant profile.

Emotional Distance

One of the most noticeable characteristics of avoidants is their tendency to maintain an emotional distance in relationships. This distance is not necessarily a lack of affection, but rather a strategy to avoid pain and vulnerability.

Avoidants may appear cold or distanti, preferendo non mostrare i loro veri sentimenti per paura di essere feriti.

Self-sufficiency

Avoidants consider themselves highly self-sufficient. This behavior stems from the need not to depend on others for emotional support, a strategy developed in childhood. Self-reliance can lead them to avoid asking for help or support, even when they need it, and to handle difficulties on their own.

Fear of Intimacy

Emotional intimacy poses a threat to avoidants. They fear that opening up too much could lead to rejection or abandonment. As a result, they can avoid situations that require vulnerability, keeping relationships at a superficial level. This fear of intimacy often makes it difficult for them to build deep and meaningful relationships.

Impairment of Relationships

Avoidants tend to downplay the importance of emotional relationships. They may focus more on practical aspects of life, such as work or hobbies, to avoid confronting their emotional fears. This devaluation of relationships is a defence against the risk of being emotionally dependent on others.

Contradictory behaviour's

Despite the desire to maintain emotional distance, avoidants may exhibit contradictory behaviours. They may seek closeness when they feel insecure, only to withdraw again when the relationship becomes too intimate. This cycle of getting closer and farther apart can be confusing and frustrating for their partners.

Controlling Emotions

Avoidants tend to strictly control their emotions. They have difficulty expressing intense feelings, both positive and negative. This emotional control is a strategy to avoid pain, but it can also prevent them from fully experiencing emotional experiences.

Superficial Relationships

Because of their fear of intimacy and emotional control, avoidants often form superficial relationships. These relationships lack depth and authenticity and can be unsatisfying for both them and their partners. Avoidants may have many acquaintances, but few close friends.

Understanding the profile of an avoidant is essential to begin the process of change. Recognizing these characteristics and behaviours allows you to see beyond the surface and begin to work on the roots of these patterns. In the next few chapters, we will explore how to transform these behaviour's and build deeper, more meaningful relationships. Mindfulness is the first step toward a richer and more emotionally fulfilling life.

1.3 Differences From Other Attachment Styles

To fully understand avoidant attachment, it is helpful to compare it to other attachment styles identified by attachment theory. Each style represents a unique way of interacting with the world and relationships, influenced by childhood experiences with key role models. Let's look at the key differences between avoidant attachment and other attachment styles: secure, anxious, and disorganized.

Secure Attachment

Secure attachment is characterized by a balance between independence and closeness. People with this style are comfortable with intimacy and vulnerability, thanks to positive and stable childhood experiences. Children with secure attachment received consistent and loving care, developing a fundamental trust in their role models. As adults, these individuals can form deep and meaningful relationships, effectively managing stress and relationship difficulties.

In contrasto, gli evitanti mantengono una distanza emotiva per evitare la vulnerability. While secure individuals welcome and value emotional relationships, avoidants downplay them, seeing them as potentially risky.

Anxious attachment

Anxious attachment, also known as anxious-ambivalent attachment, manifests itself in individuals who yearn intensely for closeness but fear rejection and abandonment. These people often exhibit needy and worried behaviors, constantly seeking reassurance and approval. As children, they had inconsistent role models, who sometimes responded to their needs and other times did not, creating a sense of uncertainty.

While avoidants avoid intimacy, anxious people desperately seek it. This dichotomy represents one of the fundamental differences between these two styles. Avoidants prefer self-sufficiency and distance, while anxious people continually seek contact and confirmation.

Disorganized Attachment

Disorganized attachment is characterized by a mix of anxious and avoidant behaviours. Individuals with this style may exhibit contradictory and disoriented reactions in relationships, alternating between seeking closeness and avoidance behaviours. These individuals have often had traumatic childhood experiences or frightening role models, creating an unstable foundation for emotional development.

People with disorganized attachment may have behaviours like those of avoidants in terms of emotional distance, but their reaction is often less predictable and more chaotic. The presence of trauma adds a level of complexity that clearly sets this style apart from others.

Understanding the Differences

Recognizing the differences between the various attachment styles is essential to understanding one's relationship dynamics. Each style brings with it unique challenges, but also opportunities for growth. While avoidant attachment may seem like an insurmountable obstacle, it is possible to transform these patterns through mindfulness and commitment.

Comparing ourselves to other attachment styles gives us a broader perspective, helping us to see that we are not alone in our struggles. Each style represents an adaptive response to a particular environment, and understanding these responses allows us to begin to change.

With a deeper understanding of the differences between attachment styles, we can begin to work on ourselves, developing healthier and more satisfying relationships. This journey takes time and patience, but with determination and support, it is possible to transform our emotional lives.

As we read on, we'll discover how to apply this knowledge in daily practice, addressing the challenges of avoidant attachment, and building a future of authentic and meaningful connections.

Chapter 2: Real Life Stories

Personal experiences offer insight into the dynamics of avoidant attachment. Through authentic testimonies, we can better understand the challenges and triumphs of those who have lived with this attachment style, providing hope and guidance to those who face similar challenges.

Mary's Childhood: The Origin of Avoidance

Maria, a 35-year-old woman, describes her childhood as a time of cold emotional distance. Growing up in a family where emotional needs were ignored, Maria learned early on to rely only on herself. Maria's mother was emotionally unavailable, often lost in her problems, while her father was physically present but emotionally absent. This environment led Maria to develop a strong sense of independence, but also a deep fear of intimacy.

In her adult relationships, Maria has maintained an emotional distance, finding it difficult to trust others. However, through therapy, she began to recognize these patterns. Her therapist taught her mindfulness techniques, which helped her live in the present and recognize her feelings without judging them. Maria learned to openly communicate her fears and work on building deeper, more meaningful relationships.

John's Struggle with Intimacy

Giovanni, a 40-year-old man, shares a similar story but with different nuances. Growing up in a family where emotional needs were often ignored; Giovanni developed a strong fear of vulnerability. As a child, any attempt to seek affection or understanding was rejected or ignored, leading him to conclude that the only way to avoid pain was to avoid intimacy.

As an adult, John avoided deep relationships, preferring to be alone rather than risk being hurt. These behaviors led him to increasing isolation, which negatively affected his social and work life. A turning point came when John decided to participate in a support group for people with attachment problems. Through comparison with other people who shared his same fears, Giovanni began to explore his feelings and build more authentic connections.

Laura's Transformation: From Rejection to Healing

Laura, a 28-year-old young woman, recounts how her childhood was marked by frequent emotional rejection from her parents. This led her to develop a defence mechanism that kept her safe from being hurt but also prevented her from experiencing fulfilling relationships. Laura described how whenever a relationship became too intimate, she felt an overwhelming urge to escape.

The change began when Laura met with a therapist who specializes in attachment. Through regular sessions, she learned to recognize her avoidance patterns and confront her fears. Therapy has provided her with tools to manage intimacy-related anxiety and to build more balanced relationships. Today, Laura is in a stable relationship and has learned to express her emotional needs without fear.

Couple Experiences: The Challenge and Growth Together

Not only are individual experiences relevant, but also those of couples where one or both partners have an avoidant attachment. Marco and Anna, who have been married for ten years, have struggled for a long time with the dynamics of their attachment. Marco, with an avoidant attachment, tended to withdraw emotionally, while Anna, with an anxious attachment, constantly sought reassurance.

Their relationship reached a breaking point, prompting them to seek a couple's therapy. Through counselling, they learned to understand each other's attachment styles and develop strategies to better communicate and meet each other's needs. Marco worked on his fear of intimacy, while Anna learned to manage her anxiety without overpowering Marco. This path has led them to greater understanding and intimacy, transforming their relationship.

Hope Through Awareness

Testimonials show that change is possible. Through mindfulness and commitment, you can transform avoidant attachment patterns and build more fulfilling relationships. Therapy, support groups, and mindfulness techniques are powerful tools that can help in this process. The stories of Maria, Giovanni, Laura, Marco, and Anna are proof that, despite the challenges, the path to healthy and meaningful relationships is possible and achievable.

These experiences offer not only understanding but also hope. Through confronting difficulties and a determination to change, everyone can find their own path to emotional healing. Real-life stories remind us that we are not alone in our struggles and that, with the right support, we can overcome emotional barriers and live a life filled with authentic and fulfilling connections.

2.1 Experiences and Testimonies: Personal Accounts of Those Who Have Experienced Avoidant Attachment

The experiences and testimonies of those who have experienced avoidant attachment offer a valuable and real-world insight into the challenges and triumphs encountered along the path of growth and healing. These personal accounts not only illuminate the common difficulties associated with avoidant attachment but also provide inspiration and hope for those who are trying to overcome similar issues.

Tales of Isolation and Loneliness

Many individuals with avoidant attachment describe deep feelings of isolation and loneliness. For example, Anna, a 28-year-old young woman, recounts how her childhood, characterized by emotionally distant parents, shaped her tendency to withdraw emotionally into adult relationships. Often feeling misunderstood and unable to express her emotional needs, Anna found it difficult to build deep connections with others.

Anna's example:

Anna shares that whenever a relationship started to get serious, she felt the need to withdraw. This behavior has led to the breakup of many promising relationships, leaving her with a sense of guilt and frustration. It was not until therapy that she began to understand and deal with these patterns, gradually learning to trust and connect with others.

Overcoming the Fear of Rejection

Fear of rejection is a recurring theme among those who struggle with avoidant attachment. Marco, a 35-year-old man, describes how the fear of rejection led him to avoid emotional intimacy. Whenever he perceived the possibility of rejection, he withdrew into himself, preferring loneliness to vulnerability.

Mark's example:

Marco began a journey of self-understanding by reading books on attachment and participating in support groups. These resources have provided him with tools to deal with his fear of rejection and to begin building relationships based on trust. Her story is a powerful example of how education and community support can turn fear into strength.

Stories of Transformation and Healing

Testimonies of transformation and healing offer hope and show that change is possible. Clara, a 42-year-old woman, tells how, through intensive care, she was able to transform her attachment style from avoidant to secure.

Example of Clara:

Clara describes how therapy helped her identify the roots of her avoidant attachment to the family dynamics of her childhood. Through therapeutic work, she has learned to recognize and express her emotional needs, developing healthier and more satisfying relationships. Her story is a powerful reminder that, with commitment and support, healing is possible.

The Power of Support and Sharing

Sharing experiences with others facing similar challenges can be extraordinarily powerful. Participating in support groups or online communities provides a sense of belonging and understanding, which is crucial to the healing process.

Example of a Support Group:

Giulia, a participant in a support group, talks about how sharing her experiences with other people with avoidant attachment has helped her feel less alone and find new strategies to cope with her challenges. The empathy and mutual support within the group had a transformative impact on her life.

The experiences and testimonies of people who have experienced avoidant attachment show that despite the difficulties, it is possible to find healing and build healthier relationships. These tales offer hope and guidance to those who are still in the process of facing and overcoming their emotional challenges. Sharing experiences, therapeutic support and personal commitment are key to transformation and well-being.

2.2 Overcoming Loneliness and Rejection

Loneliness and rejection are common experiences for those living with an avoidant attachment. These feelings can become deep scars that affect relationships and emotional well-being. However, there are strategies and approaches that can help overcome these difficulties, leading to a more fulfilling life and more meaningful relationships.

Emotional loneliness

Emotional loneliness is a condition in which a person feels a lack of connection and understanding, even though they may have many social interactions. For those with an avoidant attachment, this loneliness is often self-imposed as a defined mechanism against vulnerability. However, prolonged loneliness can lead to feelings of depression and anxiety.

1. **Strategies** for Overcoming Loneliness
2. **Mindfulness and Acceptance:** The first step in overcoming loneliness is to acknowledge and accept it. Often, those with avoidant attachments ignore or minimize their feelings. Mindfulness can be a powerful tool for increasing awareness of one's emotional state without judgment.
3. **Cultivating Authentic Relationships:** It is important to seek out relationships that allow for an authentic connection. This can mean starting slowly, sharing small personal details, and gradually building trust. Seeking out safe environments, such as supportive groups or sympathetic circles of friends, can facilitate this process.
4. **Vulnerability Practice:** Being vulnerable can be scary, but it's essential for building deep relationships. Starting with small acts of vulnerability, such as expressing your feelings or asking for help, can help build confidence in yourself and others.
5. **Therapy:** Collaborating with a therapist can provide a safe space to explore and understand the root causes of loneliness. Therapy can provide tools and strategies for coping with and overcoming these feelings.

Dealing with Rejection

Rejection is a painful experience that can strengthen the desire to avoid intimacy. Those with an avoidant attachment may see rejection as a confirmation of their fears, leading them to withdraw further.

1. **Recognize Rejection as Part of Life**: It is crucial to understand that rejection is an inevitable part of life and does not necessarily reflect one's worth. Accepting this can help reduce the emotional impact of rejection.
2. **Develop a Growth Mindset: Adopting** a growth mindset, where rejection is seen as a learning opportunity rather than a condemnation, can help you better manage these experiences. Every rejection can be an opportunity to reflect and improve.
3. **Strengthen self-esteem:** Working on self-esteem can make rejection less painful. Activities such as practicing gratitude, acknowledging one's successes, and self-care can boost self-esteem and make it easier to deal with rejection.
4. **Social Support:** Having a support network can make a big difference. Friends, family, or support groups can offer understanding and comfort, helping to see rejection in a less personal, more objective light.

Transformation Through Support

The stories of people who have successfully coped with loneliness and rejection are inspiring. For example, Laura learned to overcome her fear of rejection through therapy and support from friends. Paul, through the support group, found the courage to be vulnerable and built authentic relationships.

These experiences show that, with the right support and strategies, it is possible to overcome loneliness and rejection. The key is awareness, acceptance, and a commitment to work on yourself. Through practicing mindfulness, building authentic relationships, and strengthening self-esteem, anyone can find their way to a more emotionally rich and fulfilling life.

Overcoming loneliness and rejection takes time, patience, and the right approach. Through awareness, vulnerability, and support, you can turn these negative feelings into opportunities for growth. The testimonies of those who have walked this path offer hope and show that change is possible. With commitment and determination, it is possible to build a life filled with authentic and fulfilling relationships.

2.3 Transformation and Healing

Overcoming problems related to avoidant attachment requires a path of personal transformation and emotional healing. The testimonies of those who have gone through this process show that, with commitment and support, it is possible to change patterns of behavior and build a more fulfilling life.

Elena's Path of Transformation

Elena, a 38-year-old woman, has lived most of her life avoiding close relationships. Growing up in a family where emotions were seen as a weakness, Elena learned not to rely on others and to hide her true feelings. However, this attitude led her to feel deeply lonely and unfulfilled.

The turning point for Elena came when she started a path of therapy. Her therapist helped her understand the roots of her avoidant attachment and recognize how it negatively affected her life. Through therapy, Elena learned to confront her fears and develop new strategies for managing relationships.

Tools for Healing

Mindfulness and Meditation: These practices help you develop awareness of your emotional states and live in the present. Daily meditation can reduce anxiety and improve your ability to connect with others.

Cognitive-Behavioral Therapy (CBT): CBT is effective in modifying dysfunctional thoughts and behaviors. It helps to identify negative thoughts related to relationships and replace them with more positive and realistic thoughts.

Support Groups: Participating in support groups provides a safe environment to share experiences and receive support. This can reduce feelings of isolation and provide new tools to deal with challenges.

Gradual Exposure Exercises: Gradually addressing situations that cause intimacy-related anxiety can help desensitize these fears. Starting with small steps and progressively increasing the level of exposure can be very effective.

Luca's Story: From Rejection to Connection

Luca, 42, has always feared rejection, which has led him to avoid intimate relationships. After many disappointments, he decided to change. Through therapy, she learned to recognize her negative thought patterns and replace them with healthier approaches. He also participated in workshops on emotional communication, which provided him with tools to express his feelings more effectively.

Luca began practicing mindfulness, which helped him stay present in his interactions and reduce anxiety. Over time, she built more meaningful relationships and found the courage to be vulnerable. Her story is an example of how determination and the use of therapeutic tools can lead to profound transformation.

Healing Through Self-Acceptance

A crucial element in the healing journey is self-acceptance. Those with an avoidant attachment often have low self-esteem and tend to judge themselves harshly. Working on your self-esteem and learning to accept yourself for who you are can make a significant difference.

Self-compassion: Learning to treat yourself with kindness and understanding, as you would be a friend, can significantly improve your self-esteem.

Acknowledge Your Progress: By celebrating small successes and acknowledging the progress you have made, you can build greater self-confidence.

Positive Visualizations: Using visualization techniques to imagine positive and fulfilling situations can help you change your perception of yourself and your relationship skills.

Stories of transformation and healing show that despite initial difficulties, it is possible to overcome avoidant attachment patterns and build an emotionally satisfying life. With commitment, therapeutic support, and the use of appropriate tools, it is possible to reconnect with others and experience deeper, more authentic relationships. The key is awareness, self-acceptance, and a determination to change. These stories remind us that we are not alone in our journey and that, with the right support, every challenge can be overcome.

Chapter 3: The Science of Attachment

Attachment is a complex phenomenon that has its roots in biology and psychology. Attachment theory, formulated by John Bowlby, is based on the idea that the emotional bonds we form in childhood with our caregivers profoundly affect our development and future relationships. Neuroscientific research has shown how these early attachment experiences affect the brain, especially in areas responsible for emotional regulation and stress response.

Studies have shown that children with secure attachment tend to have better emotional and social development. In contrast, those with avoidant attachment often show difficulties in managing emotions and interpersonal relationships. These children learn early on to suppress their emotional needs as a strategy of adaptation to an environment where their requests for affection and support are ignored or rejected.

Research on brain plasticity has revealed that the brain continues to develop and change in response to experiences, even in adulthood. This means that although attachment patterns formed in childhood may be deeply ingrained, it is possible to modify them through new experiences and therapeutic practices.

One of the most powerful tools for understanding attachment is the use of functional magnetic resonance imaging (MRI), which allows us to observe how different areas of the brain are activated in response to emotional stimuli. MRI studies have shown that people with avoidant attachment tend to have less activation in areas of the brain associated with empathy and emotion regulation, such as the amygdala and prefrontal cortex.

In addition, research has explored the role of neurotransmitters, such as oxytocin and dopamine, in attachment. Oxytocin, often called the "love hormone," plays a crucial role in the formation of social bonds and affectivity. Studies have suggested that reduced oxytocin levels may be associated with difficulties in attachment and the formation of intimate relationships.

Longitudinal research has also shown that attachment formed in childhood has lasting effects on the individual's development. Children who have experienced secure attachment tend to develop greater emotional resilience, while those with avoidant attachment may face greater difficulties in relationships and emotional regulation.

However, despite these challenges, neuroplasticity offers hope. Through targeted therapeutic interventions, such as cognitive-behavioral therapy (CBT) and attachment-focused therapy, dysfunctional attachment patterns can be restructured. These interventions help people develop new ways of relating and improve their ability to connect emotionally with others.

Finally, research continues to explore new ways to support people on their journey to healing from avoidant attachment. Emerging techniques, such as mindfulness and compassion-based therapy, are proving to be effective in promoting emotional awareness and the ability to build healthier, more fulfilling relationships.

In summary, the science of attachment offers a deep understanding of the biological and psychological roots of our relational behaviors. This knowledge equips us with the necessary tools to embark on a path of personal transformation and improve the quality of our relationships. The road to healing can be long and challenging, but research shows us that change is possible and that, with the right support, we can develop stronger, more authentic emotional bonds.

3.1 Neuroscientific Foundations of Attachment

The neuroscience of attachment provides us with a detailed understanding of how our brains develop and maintain emotional bonds. John Bowlby, with his attachment theory, laid the foundations for understanding the importance of early emotional bonds in the formation of our future relationships. Modern neuroscience has expanded on these ideas, demonstrating how attachment experiences affect brain structures and functions.

Brain Development and Attachment

The human brain is highly plastic, especially during the first few years of life. Attachment experiences profoundly affect the development of brain areas responsible for emotional regulation, stress response, and socialization. Children who receive consistent and loving care develop more robust neuronal connections in areas related to emotional safety and trust. In contrast, children with inconsistent or negative attachment experiences tend to develop more pronounced stress responses and defense mechanisms that may persist into adulthood.

Amygdala and Stress Response

The amygdala, a small, almond-shaped structure in the brain, is critical for the response to stress and fear. In children with avoidant attachment, the amygdala may be overactive, leading to increased sensitivity to emotional threats. This hyperactivation can contribute to avoidance behaviors and difficulty forming secure emotional bonds.

Prefrontal Cortex and Emotional Regulation

The prefrontal cortex participates in the regulation of emotions and the control of impulsive behaviors. Positive attachment experiences promote the development of a well-integrated prefrontal cortex, capable of modulating emotional responses effectively. Conversely, a dysfunctional attachment can lead to difficulties in emotional regulation, making it more difficult to manage stress and intense emotions.

Oxytocin: The Attachment Hormone

Oxytocin, often called the "love hormone," plays a crucial role in the formation of social bonds and affectivity. This chemical is released in copious amounts during childbirth, breastfeeding, and affectionate interactions. Studies have shown that elevated oxytocin levels are associated with secure attachment behaviors, while reduced levels may be related to difficulties in attachment and the formation of intimate relationships.

Brain Plasticity and the Potential for Change

One of the most promising aspects of attachment neuroscience is the concept of brain plasticity, which refers to the brain's ability to change and adapt in response to new experiences. This means that even though attachment patterns formed in childhood may be deeply ingrained, it is possible to modify them through new experiences and therapeutic interventions. Cognitive behavioral therapy (CBT), attachment-focused therapy, and mindfulness are effective tools for restructuring dysfunctional attachment patterns and promoting greater emotional security.

Functional Magnetic Resonance Imaging (MRI) and Brain Studies

The use of functional magnetic resonance imaging (MRI) has made it possible to observe in real time how the brain responds to emotional stimuli. MRI studies have revealed that people with avoidant attachment show less activation in areas of the brain associated with empathy and emotion regulation. This data provides a visual and tangible understanding of how attachment experiences shape brain functioning.

The neuroscience of attachment gives us insight into how early experiences affect our emotional and relational development. Understanding these mechanisms allows us to recognize the importance of early life experiences and to use targeted therapeutic interventions to promote change and healing.

With the help of science, we can work to transform our attachment patterns and build more secure and satisfying relationships.

3.2 The Influence of Childhood on Adult Attachment Style

Childhood experiences play a crucial role in determining the attachment style we develop as adults. Attachment theory, formulated by John Bowlby, highlights how early emotional bonds with our caregivers profoundly influence our psychological development and future relationships.

Importance of First Relationships

During the first few years of life, children form bonds of attachment with their primary caregivers. Not only do these bonds provide security and comfort, but they also shape how children perceive and interact with the world. If a child receives consistent, loving, and responsive care, they are likely to develop a secure attachment, characterized by trust in relationships and their own ability to be loved.

Conversely, if care is inconsistent, detached, or rejective, the child may develop an insecure attachment style, which may be anxious, avoidant, or disorganized. These insecure attachment styles can lead to emotional and relational difficulties that persist into adulthood.

Avoidant Attachment: Origins and Consequences

Children who develop an avoidant attachment often have caregivers who are emotionally unavailable or rejective. Faced with these experiences, the child soon learns to suppress his emotional needs as a survival strategy. This defense mechanism becomes an ingrained behavioral pattern, leading the individual to avoid intimacy and maintain emotional distance in adult relationships.

The consequences of an avoidant attachment can include difficulties forming and maintaining close relationships, trust issues, low self-esteem, and a tendency to avoid situations that require emotional vulnerability. Adults with avoidant attachment may appear self-sufficient and independent, but they often struggle internally with feelings of loneliness and insecurity.

Longitudinal Studies and Empirical Evidence

Numerous longitudinal studies have confirmed the influence of early attachment experiences on adult development. For example, research conducted by Mary Ainsworth through the "Strange Situation" experiment identified various attachment styles in children and demonstrated how these styles predict future behaviors in relationships.

Further studies followed children from infancy through adulthood, showing that those who had developed a secure attachment were more likely to build stable and satisfying relationships, while those with avoidant or anxious attachment faced greater emotional and relational difficulties.

Moderating Factors and Possibilities for Change

It's important to note that while early attachment experiences are influential, they don't irrevocably determine our relationship destiny. Moderating factors such as social support, positive afterward experiences, and access to therapeutic resources can mitigate the negative effects of an insecure attachment.

Brain plasticity and the ability to learn continuously offer possibilities for change. Through therapy and other forms of intervention, it is possible to restructure attachment patterns and develop new ways of relating. For example, attachment-focused therapy and cognitive-behavioural therapy can help people recognize and change their dysfunctional behaviours patterns.

Childhood experiences have a profound impact on the development of attachment styles, influencing how we perceive ourselves and others. However, with the proper mindfulness and support, it is possible to overcome insecure attachment patterns and build healthier, more satisfying relationships. Understanding the roots of our behaviours allows us to embark on a path of healing and personal growth, paving the way for a richer and more emotionally fulfilling life

3.3 Recent Studies and Research

Attachment research has continued to evolve, offering new insights and corroboration to existing theories. Recent studies have used advanced technologies and innovative methodologies to explore in greater depth the dynamics of attachment and their impact on psychological and relational development.

Neuroimaging Technologies

The use of neuroimaging technologies, such as functional magnetic resonance imaging (MRI), has allowed scientists to directly observe the brain activities associated with different attachment styles. These studies revealed that individuals with secure attachment show increased activity in areas of the brain related to emotion regulation and empathy, such as the prefrontal cortex and amygdala. Conversely, those who have avoidant attachment tend to show reduced activation in these areas, indicating a lower ability to manage emotions and connect empathically with others.

Genetics and Epigenetics

Genetic and epigenetic research has explored how genes and the environment interact to influence attachment development. Studies have identified genetic variants that may predispose individuals to certain attachment styles, but have also highlighted how environmental experiences, such as the support and care received during childhood, can modify the expression of these genes through epigenetic mechanisms. This suggests that, despite a genetic predisposition, attachment can be influenced and modified by life experiences.

Attachment and Mental Health

A significant area of recent research focuses on the link between attachment and mental health. Studies have shown that insecure attachment styles, such as avoidant attachment, are associated with a higher risk of developing mental disorders, including depression, anxiety, and post-traumatic stress disorder (PTSD). Understanding these links has led to the development of specific therapeutic interventions that aim to improve attachment security as a means of promoting mental health.

Innovative Therapeutic Interventions

The continuous evolution of therapeutic approaches has led to the development of innovative interventions for the treatment of attachment problems. Attachment-focused therapy, mentalization-based therapy, and emotion-focused therapy are some of the methodologies that have been shown to be effective in improving attachment security and promoting healthier relationships.

Attachment Focused Therapy (AFT): This form of therapy focuses on exploring past and present relationships to understand and change attachment patterns. The goal is to help individuals develop a greater awareness of their emotional experiences and improve the quality of their relationships.

Mentalization-Based Therapy (MBT): MBT helps individuals develop the ability to understand their own mental states and those of others. This ability, called mentalization, is crucial for building and maintaining healthy and secure relationships.

Emotion-Focused Therapy (EFT): EFT works directly with emotions to help individuals recognize, express, and regulate their feelings. This approach can be especially helpful for those who struggle with avoidant attachment, as it helps them develop a greater capacity for emotional connection.

Longitudinal Studies and Prevention

Longitudinal studies continue to provide valuable data on attachment developmental pathways. These studies follow individuals and families over time, looking at how childhood experiences affect long-term psychological and relational development. The results of these studies are crucial for developing prevention and early intervention programs, aimed at promoting secure attachment from childhood.

Recent research has broadened our understanding of attachment, confirmed the importance of early life experiences and offered new therapeutic perspectives. Using advanced technologies and interdisciplinary approaches, scientists continue to explore the complexities of attachment, opening new avenues for the prevention and treatment of relationship problems. This growing body of knowledge brings us closer to a more comprehensive understanding and more effective solutions to improve attachment security and emotional well-being.

Chapter 4: Custom Emotional Maps

Personalized emotion maps are powerful tools for exploring and understanding your emotions and behaviors. These maps help you visualize and track the connections between events, thoughts, emotions, and reactions, giving you a clear view of your emotional patterns.

Creating Your Own Emotional Map

Creating an emotional map starts with identifying the main events and situations that elicit strong emotional reactions. These can include stressful moments, relationship conflicts, personal successes, or any other significant experience. Each event is mapped in relation to the emotions it arouses, such as fear, joy, anger, or sadness.

Once you have identified these events and the associated emotions, the next step is to analyze the thoughts and beliefs that arise in response to these emotions. For example, a conflict with a coworker could stir up anger and thoughts of insecurity or inadequacy. These thoughts and beliefs are often rooted in early life experiences and cultural and family influences.

Identifying Patterns and Triggers

Emotional maps allow us to identify recurring patterns and specific triggers that influence our emotional reactions. A trigger is anything that triggers an intense emotional response. It can be a word, a gesture, a situation, or even a thought. Identifying these triggers is crucial for understanding why we react in certain ways and for developing strategies to better manage our emotions.

For example, if we notice that a certain type of criticism always provokes a defensive or angry reaction, we can start working on understanding this trigger. Perhaps criticism harkens back past experiences of rejection or judgment, and acknowledging this connection may be the first step toward a more balanced and conscious response.

Using the Personal Growth Map

Once we have a clear map of our emotional patterns and triggers, we can use it for personal growth. This process involves several steps:

1. **Recognition and Acceptance:** Accepting your feelings and thoughts without judgment is crucial. Mindfulness and other mindfulness techniques can be especially helpful at this stage.
2. **Cognitive Restructuring:** Working on the thoughts and beliefs that emerge in response to triggers. Cognitive-behavioral therapy (CBT) is an effective approach to modifying dysfunctional thoughts and replacing them with more balanced and realistic ones.
3. **New Strategy Development:** Create and implement new strategies to manage triggers and emotions in a healthier way. This can include relaxation techniques, breathing exercises, meditation, and the use of social support.
4. **Monitoring and Review:** Continue to monitor your reactions and review the emotional map for updates. Personal growth is an ongoing process, and emotional maps need to be reviewed and adapted as new understandings and skills are developed.

Testimonials and Successes

The testimonials of those who have used emotional maps for their personal growth are often very positive. For example, Sara, a 30-year-old woman, found that the emotional map helped her better understand her anxiety reactions and develop more effective strategies for managing them. Marco, 45, has used emotional maps to improve his work relationships, recognizing and addressing his critic-related triggers.

Personalized emotion maps are powerful tools for understanding and transforming one's emotional patterns. Through the creation and use of these maps, you can identify triggers, work on dysfunctional thoughts and beliefs, and develop strategies for healthier emotional management. Awareness and commitment to the process of personal growth can lead to a more balanced and fulfilling life, improving not only individual well-being but also the quality of interpersonal relationships.

4.1 Creating Your Own Emotional Map

Creating a personal emotional map is a process that requires introspection and reflection. This map serves as a tool for identifying, understanding, and visualizing your emotional patterns, allowing you to see how different experiences and thoughts affect your emotional reactions.

Step 1: Collect Meaningful Experiences

The first step in creating an emotional map is to collect all the significant experiences that elicit strong emotions. These events can be stressful situations, moments of conflict, personal successes, or everyday experiences that particularly affect you. Write down these events and try to be as detailed as possible, including the context and people involved.

Step 2: Identify Emotions

For each experience you recorded, identify the main emotions you felt. Use precise language to describe emotions, going beyond generic terms like "happy" or "sad." More specific terms such as "frustrated," "anxious," "Enthusiastic," or "disappointed" will help you understand your emotional response better.

Step 3: Analyze Your Thoughts and Beliefs

Once you've identified your emotions, the next step is to analyze the thoughts and beliefs that accompany them. These may include judgments about yourself, others, or the situation in general. For example, if you experienced anxiety during a presentation at work, you may find that your thoughts included fears of failure or negative judgments from colleagues.

Step 4: View Connections

Now that you've identified the associated experiences, emotions, and thoughts, it's time to visualize the connections between them. You can do this by drawing a map that shows how each experience is connected to specific emotions and thoughts. Use different arrows and colours to represent the relationships between the elements. For example, you could use red to indicate negative emotions and green for positive ones, with arrows linking experiences to their emotional and cognitive effects.

Step 5: Recognize Triggers

During the process of creating your emotional map, pay attention to triggers – the situations, words, or behaviours that trigger your emotional reactions. Recognizing these triggers is crucial for developing emotional management strategies. Once you've located them, write them down clearly on the map, trying to identify if there are any recurring patterns.

Step 6: Reflect and Adapt

The emotion map is a dynamic tool that should be updated and reviewed regularly. Periodically reflecting on your experiences and adding new information will help keep the map current and relevant. Use the map to identify areas for improvement and to track your progress over time.

Creating a personal emotional map is a process of self-reflection that can lead to a greater awareness of one's emotional and behavioural patterns. This tool helps you visualize and understand the connections between experiences, emotions, and thoughts, providing you with a solid foundation for developing effective emotional management strategies. With time and effort, the emotional map can become a valuable resource for your journey of personal growth and emotional well-being.

4.2 Identifying Patterns and Triggers

Identifying your emotional patterns and the triggers that trigger them is a key step in improving your emotional management and developing greater self-awareness. This process requires attention and thought, but it offers valuable tools to better understand your reactions and adopt more effective strategies.

Analysis of Emotional Patterns

Emotional patterns are recurring patterns of thoughts, emotions, and behaviors that occur in response to certain situations. These patterns can be both positive and negative, and they profoundly affect how we relate to ourselves and others. To identify your emotional patterns, it is helpful to follow these steps:

Observation of Reactions: Pay attention to how you react emotionally in different situations. Write down your immediate emotional responses and the thoughts that accompany them. Try to do this without judgment, simply by observing what is going on inside you.

Event Recording: Keep a journal of your emotional experiences. Each day, it takes a few minutes to write down the meaningful situations you experienced and the emotions you felt. This will help you identify patterns that recur over time.

Reflection on Behaviors: Examine the behaviors you engage in in response to your emotions. For example, do you tend to avoid certain situations when you're anxious? Or do you react aggressively when you feel threatened? Recognizing these behaviors is crucial to understanding how you manage your emotions.

Identifying Triggers

Triggers are specific stimuli that trigger an intense emotional response. They can be external (such as a situation or word) or internal (such as a thought or memory). Identifying your triggers is key to developing more effective emotional management strategies. Here's how to do it:

Recognize Triggering Situations: Reflect on situations that tend to elicit strong emotional reactions. For example, you may notice that criticism at work triggers feelings of anger or that conflicts with partners evoke anxiety. Writing down these situations helps you become more aware of triggers.

Explore Associated Thoughts: Once you've identified your triggers, analyse the thoughts that accompany them. Often, emotional triggers are related to deep beliefs about oneself or others. For example, criticism might trigger the thought "I'm not good enough," which in turn generates anger or self-doubt.

Identify Physical Signals: Intense emotional responses are often accompanied by physical cues such as muscle tension, rapid heartbeat, or sweating. Learning to recognize these physical cues can help you identify triggers before emotions become overwhelming.

Analyse Emotions: The emotions triggered by triggers can vary in intensity and duration. Taking note of specific emotions and their intensity will help you better understand your emotional responses. For example, you may find that mild criticism evokes mild irritation, while severe criticism provokes intense anger.

Using Triggers for Personal Growth

Once you've identified your emotional patterns and triggers, you can use them as tools for personal growth. Here are some strategies to do so:

Developing Emotional Regulation Techniques: Learning emotional regulation techniques, such as deep breathing, meditation, or positive self-talk, can help you better manage your emotional responses to triggers.

Response Planning: Preparing alternative responses to triggers can reduce the intensity of your emotional reactions. For example, if you know that criticism triggers anger in you, you can plan to respond calmly and ask for clarification rather than reacting impulsively.

Creating a Supportive Environment: Surrounding yourself with people who understand and support your emotional growth journey can make a big difference. Talking about your triggers with trusted friends or a therapist can give you new perspectives and strategies for managing them.

Mindfulness Practice: Mindfulness is an effective practice for developing greater awareness of one's thoughts, emotions, and reactions. Practicing mindfulness regularly can help you stay present and respond to triggers with greater calmness and clarity.

Identifying and understanding your emotional patterns and triggers is a critical step in improving your emotional management and developing greater selfawareness. Using this information, you can create effective strategies to address triggers and promote personal growth. Awareness and commitment to this process can lead to a more emotionally balanced and fulfilling life, improving not only individual well-being but also the quality of interpersonal relationships.

4.3 Using the Personal Growth Map

Once you've created and identified the patterns and triggers through your emotional map, it's essential to actively use it to foster personal growth. The map is not just an exercise in introspection, but a dynamic tool that can guide you towards better emotion management and healthier relationships.

Steps to Use the Emotional Map

Acknowledgment and Acceptance:

Mindfulness: Use the map to increase awareness of your emotional patterns. Acknowledging that these patterns exist is the first step toward change.

Acceptance: Accept your feelings without judging them. Mindfulness can be especially helpful here, helping you observe your emotions without being overwhelmed by them.

Cognitive Restructuring:

Identify Dysfunctional Thoughts: Use the map to pinpoint dysfunctional thoughts that come up in response to triggers.

Replace with Positive Thoughts: Replace these thoughts with more balanced and realistic alternatives. Cognitive-behavioural therapy (CBT) offers helpful techniques for this restructuring.

Development of New Strategies:

Emotional Regulation Techniques: Implement emotional regulation techniques such as deep breathing, meditation, or positive self-talk. These tools help you manage intense emotions in a healthier way.

Response Scheduling: Prepare alternative responses to your triggers. If you know that a certain behaviour triggers a negative emotional reaction, plan for a calmer and more reflective response.

Monitoring and Review:

Emotional journaling: Keep an emotional journal to track your reactions and progress over time. Write down the situations, emotions, and how you responded. This helps you see improvements and identify areas that need further work.

Regular Updates: Review and update your emotional map regularly. Personal growth is an ongoing process, and the map should evolve with you.

Social and Therapeutic Support:

Sharing: Share your emotional map with people you trust, such as close friends, family, or a therapist. Their feedback can offer new perspectives and further support.

Therapeutic: Consider working with a therapist who can help you interpret the map and develop personalized strategies for emotional growth.

Benefits of the Emotional Map

The active use of the emotional map offers numerous benefits:

Increased Awareness: Helps develop a deeper understanding of one's emotions and behaviours.

Improved Emotional Management: Provides tools and strategies to better manage intense emotions and triggers.

Healthier Relationships: Improving emotional awareness and managing emotions can lead to more balanced and satisfying relationships.

Personal Growth: It fosters a continuous path of personal growth, helping to become more resilient and adaptable.

Success Stories

Many have found that the use of emotional maps has had a transformative impact on their lives. For example, Alessandra, a young professional, used her emotional map to deal with performance anxiety. By monitoring her triggers and working on restructuring her thoughts, she developed more self-confidence and improved her work performance.

Marco, a 50-year-old manager, has used the emotional map to improve his family relationships. By identifying triggers related to family dynamics and developing new communication strategies, she found more effective ways to connect with her children and partner.

Using the emotional map for personal growth is an ongoing process that requires awareness, reflection, and commitment. Through pattern recognition, restructuring thoughts, and developing new strategies, you can better manage your emotions and build healthier, more satisfying relationships. With time and practice, the emotional map can become a valuable ally in your personal growth journey, improving your emotional well-being and the quality of your interactions

Chapter 5: Mindfulness and Presence Techniques

Mindfulness and presence techniques are powerful tools for improving self-awareness and managing emotions. These practices, rooted in ancient meditative traditions and backed by modern research, can help you live more fully and mindfully, reducing stress and improving emotional well-being.

Fundamentals of Mindfulness

Mindfulness, or mindfulness, is the practice of intentionally bringing attention to the present moment, without judgment. This practice involves awareness of bodily sensations, thoughts, and emotions, and always encourages complete presence. Jon Kabat-Zinn, one of the pioneers of mindfulness in the Western context, defines mindfulness as "the awareness that emerges by paying attention, intentionally, to the present moment, in a non-judgmental way."

Benefits of Mindfulness

Numerous studies have shown the benefits of mindfulness for mental and physical health. Regular mindfulness practice can reduce symptoms of stress, anxiety, and depression, improve sleep quality, and increase overall well-being. Additionally, mindfulness can improve the ability to concentrate, emotional regulation, and resilience.

Practical Mindfulness Exercises

There are various practical mindfulness exercises that can be integrated into daily life. Some of the most effective include:

Breath Meditation: Focus on the breath, observing the inhalation and exhalation without trying to change it. This exercise can be practiced for a few minutes a day to increase awareness of the present moment.

Body Scan: A practice that involves bringing mindful attention to different parts of the body, from head to toe, noticing sensations without judgment. This can help you develop greater body awareness and relax.

Mindful Eating: Mindful eating, paying attention to the flavours, textures, and sensations associated with food. This exercise can improve your relationship with food and promote healthier eating.

Mindful Walking: Walking slowly, paying attention to each step, the sensations in your feet and legs, and your surroundings. This can be an effective way to integrate mindfulness into your daily life.

Guided Meditation: Listen to recordings of guided meditations that can help you focus your attention and develop mindfulness. There are many apps and online resources that offer guided meditations for various purposes.

Applications of Mindfulness in Daily Life

Mindfulness is not just a formal practice, but it can be integrated into many daily activities. For example, you can practice mindfulness while showering, paying attention to the sensations of water on your skin, or while washing dishes, focusing on the sensations of your hands and water. Every moment can become an opportunity for awareness.

Mindfulness and Relationships

Mindfulness can also improve interpersonal relationships. Being present and aware during interactions with others can improve communication, increase empathy, and reduce conflict. Practicing mindful listening, where you listen to the other person without interrupting or judging, can strengthen bonds and create a deeper connection.

Challenges of Mindfulness Practice

Like any skill, mindfulness requires practice and patience. Many find it difficult to stay focused or get frustrated when their thoughts wander. It's important to remember that mindfulness isn't about keeping a blank mind but rather noticing when the mind gets distracted and gently bringing it back to the present moment. Regular practice helps to develop this skill and overcome initial difficulties.

Mindfulness and presence techniques offer valuable tools for improving self-awareness and managing emotions. By integrating these practices into your daily life, you can reduce stress, improve mental and physical health, and build deeper, more meaningful relationships. Mindfulness is a continuous journey of exploration and growth, which can enrich every aspect of life.

5.1 Fundamentals of Mindfulness

Mindfulness is a thousand-year-old practice that has deep roots in Eastern meditation traditions, particularly Buddhism. In recent decades, this practice has been integrated into Western psychology and has gained popularity due to its proven benefits for mental health and overall well-being. Let's explore the fundamentals of mindfulness and how it can be applied to improve quality of life.

Definition of Mindfulness

Mindfulness is defined as the awareness that emerges by paying attention in a particular way: intentionally, in the present moment, and without judgment. This means being fully present in the here and now, observing your thoughts, emotions, and physical sensations without trying to change or judge them.

Key Principles of Mindfulness

Presence in the Present Moment: Mindfulness encourages you to focus on experiencing the present moment, rather than dwelling on the past or worrying about the future. This mindful presence can be applied to any daily activity, such as eating, walking, or working.

Intentionality: The practice of mindfulness is intentional. It means that you deliberately choose to pay attention consciously, rather than operating in automatic mode. This intentionality helps to develop a greater awareness of oneself and one's experiences.

Non-judgment: One of the most important aspects of mindfulness is the non-judgmental attitude towards one's thoughts and emotions. This attitude of acceptance allows you to observe your inner experiences without being overwhelmed or trapped in negative reactions.

Acceptance: Mindfulness promotes acceptance of things as they are, without trying to change them immediately. This acceptance does not mean resignation, but rather an acknowledgment of the reality of the present moment as a starting point for any future change.

Benefits of Mindfulness

Regular mindfulness practice offers numerous benefits, both mentally and physically:

Stress Reduction: Mindfulness helps reduce stress levels by teaching you to respond to difficult situations with greater calmness and clarity.

Improved Mental Health: It is effective in treating conditions such as anxiety, depression, and post-traumatic stress disorder (PTSD).

Improved Concentration: Practicing mindfulness improves the ability to concentrate and mental clarity, increasing productivity and decision-making.

Improved Relationships: Being more present and mindful in daily interactions can improve the quality of interpersonal relationships, increasing empathy and mutual understanding.

Physical Benefits: Mindfulness can help reduce stress-related physical symptoms, such as high blood pressure, gastrointestinal problems, and muscle tension.

Mindfulness Practice

Mindfulness can be practiced in many ways, adapting to individual needs and preferences. Some of the most common practices include:

Sitting Meditation: Sit in a comfortable position, close your eyes, and bring your attention to your breath. Whenever your mind wanders, gently bring your attention back to your breath.

Body Scan: Bring mindful attention to different parts of the body, noticing sensations without trying to change them.

Walking Meditation: Walking slowly, paying attention to the sensations in the feet and legs, contact with the ground and the surrounding environment.

Mindful Eating: Mindful eating, paying attention to the flavours, textures, and physical sensations associated with food.

Integrating Mindfulness into Daily Life

Mindfulness doesn't have to be limited to formal meditation sessions but can be integrated into every aspect of daily life. Some tips for practicing mindfulness during daily activities include:

During the Shower: Pay attention to the sensations of water on the skin, the sounds of running water and the physical sensations of the body.

While Washing the Dishes: Focus on the sensations of your hands in the water, the touch of the dishes, and the sound of the water.

During Conversations: Listen carefully to the other person without interrupting, noticing your internal reactions and staying present in the conversation.

Mindfulness is a versatile and accessible practice that can bring significant benefits to mental and physical health. By integrating mindfulness into your daily life, you can develop greater self-awareness, improve your emotional management, and live more fully and satisfactorily. The key is constant practice and openness to the experience of the present moment.

5.2 Practical Exercises to Raise Awareness

The practice of mindfulness can be integrated into daily life through a series of simple yet powerful exercises. These exercises help develop greater awareness of the present moment, improving stress management and the quality of personal interactions. Below are some practical mindfulness exercises that can be easily incorporated into your daily routine.

Breath Meditation

One of the fundamental mindfulness exercises is breath meditation. This simple yet effective practice can be done anywhere, anytime.

Preparation: Sit comfortably with your back straight, close your eyes and relax your body.

Focus: Bring attention to your breath. Notice the inhale and exhale, without trying to change them.

Observation: Observe how air enters and exits your body. If your mind wanders, gently bring your attention back to your breath.

Duration: Practice for at least 5-10 minutes, gradually increasing the duration as you feel more comfortable.

Body Scan

Body Scan is an exercise that helps develop greater body awareness, reducing tension and promoting relaxation.

Preparation: Lie down on a comfortable surface, close your eyes, and relax your body.

Focus: Start by bringing your attention to your feet. Notice sensations in your feet, such as temperature, contact with the ground, or any tension.

Observation: Slowly, shift your attention upward, passing through your legs, pelvis, abdomen, chest, arms, neck, and head. Observe the sensations in every part of the body.

Duration: Spend at least 20-30 minutes on this exercise, making sure to cover each part of your body carefully.

Walking Meditation

Walking meditation is a dynamic way of practicing mindfulness, ideal for those who find it difficult to sit still.

Preparation: Find a quiet path where you can walk without interruption.

Focus: Start walking slowly, paying attention to each step. Notice how your feet touch the ground, leg movement, and body balance.

Observation: Also bring attention to your surroundings, such as sounds, smells, and sights. If your mind wanders, gently bring your attention back to your body movements.

Duration: Practice for at least 10-15 minutes, allowing you to fully immerse yourself in the walking experience.

Mindful Eating

Mindful Eating is a practice that can transform the way you relate to food, improving your mindfulness and enjoyment of eating.

Preparation: Sit comfortably with your meal in front. Take a moment to observe the food, noticing the colours, shapes, and smells.

Focus: Start eating slowly, savouring every bite. Notice the textures, flavours, and sensations in the body as you chew and swallow.

Observation: Be aware of your feelings of hunger and satiety. Eat until you feel satisfied, not only physically but mentally as well.

Duration: Spend at least 20-30 minutes with your meal, avoiding distractions such as television or phones.

Guided Meditation

Guided meditation can be a great way to introduce mindfulness into your daily routine, especially if you're new to the practice.

Preparation: Find a guided meditation that you like, available on mindfulness apps, YouTube, or dedicated websites.

Focus: Follow the guide's instructions, which may include breathing exercises, visualizations, or body scans.

Note: Allow yourself to follow the guide's voice without judging your progress. Each session is an opportunity to learn and grow.

Duration: Start with short sessions of 5-10 minutes and gradually increase the duration as you get more comfortable.

Hands-on mindfulness exercises are accessible and versatile tools that can significantly improve mindfulness and well-being. By integrating these practices into daily life, you can develop a greater ability to live in the present moment, reduce stress, and improve the quality of your interpersonal relationships. With commitment and regular practice, mindfulness can become an integral part of your routine, contributing to a more balanced and fulfilling life.

5.3 Applications in Daily Life

Mindfulness can be integrated into daily life in many ways, improving overall well-being and helping to manage stress and emotions. Incorporating mindfulness into everyday activities transforms ordinary actions into mindfulness practices, making every moment an opportunity for personal growth.

Mindfulness in Daily Activities

During the Shower: Turn the shower into a mindfulness ritual. Focus on the sensations of the water on your skin, the temperature, the scent of the soap, and the sound of the water flowing. Let go of your thoughts and bring your attention to the present moment.

Washing the Dishes: Even a simple task like washing dishes can become a mindfulness exercise. Feel the warmth of the water, the soap on your hands, and the sound of dishes rubbing together. Focus your attention on these feelings and stay present.

Driving: When driving, pay attention to the feel of your hands on the wheel, the noise of the engine, and the view of the road ahead. Avoid thinking about future destinations or commitments and focus on the journey itself.

House Cleaning: Cleaning your home can be an opportunity to practice mindfulness. While vacuuming or dusting furniture, focus your attention on your physical sensations and body movements. Feel the connection between your body and the environment.

Mindfulness in Relationships

Active Listening: Practice active listening in conversations. Pay attention to what the other person is saying without interrupting or mentally formulating responses. Notice your emotional reactions and keep your focus on the other person.

Empathetic Communication: When talking to others, express your feelings and needs clearly and honestly. Use "I" instead of "you" to avoid blaming and creating conflict. For example, instead of saying, "You never listen to me," try saying, "I feel unheard when I speak."

Time Together Presence: Spend quality time with loved ones without distractions such as phones or television. Be present and enjoy the moment, observing how you feel and how you react.

Mindfulness at Work

Mindful breaks: During the workday, take short breaks to practice mindfulness. Close your eyes, take a few deep breaths, and focus on the present moment. This can reduce stress and increase focus.

Focus on Tasks: When doing a task, focus fully on it. Avoid multitasking and devote your full attention to one task at a time. This improves the quality of work and reduces errors.

Mindful Interactions: During meetings or interactions with colleagues, practice active listening and respond attentively. Being present in work interactions can improve communication and collaboration.

Mindfulness in Leisure

Mindful Exercise: Turns exercise into a mindfulness practice. Whether you're running, practicing yoga, or stretching, focus your attention on body sensations, breathing, and movements.

Hobbies and Hobbies: Spend time on your hobbies mindfully. Whether you're reading, cooking, painting, or playing an instrument, fully immerse yourself in the activity and notice how you feel.

Time in Nature: Spend time outdoors, taking a close look at the natural environment. Notice the sounds of birds, the rustling of leaves, the colours of the sky. Being in nature can profoundly improve mindfulness and well-being.

Mindfulness and Technology

Device Conscious Use: Limit the time spent on electronic devices and practice mindful use of technology. Set specific times to check emails or social media and avoid doing it compulsively.

Mindfulness Apps: Use mindfulness apps to guide your practice. There are many apps that offer guided meditations, timers, and reminders to help you stay mindful throughout the day.

Integrating mindfulness into your daily life can turn every moment into an opportunity to grow and improve your emotional well-being. Through mindful practice in daily activities, relationships, at work, and in your free time, you can live a more balanced and fulfilling life. Mindfulness is an ongoing practice that requires commitment and perseverance, but the benefits it brings are immeasurable.

Chapter 6: Conscious Communication

Mindful communication is an essential component of building and maintaining healthy and meaningful relationships. It involves not only listening attentively but also expressing oneself clearly and respectfully. Effective and mindful communication can help overcome emotional barriers, increase mutual understanding, and strengthen interpersonal bonds.

Principles of Conscious Communication

Active Listening: Active listening means giving your full attention to the other person, without interrupting or mentally making responses while the other person is talking. This type of listening demonstrates respect and genuine interest in what the other person is saying. It also involves acknowledging and reflecting on what has been said, through verbal and nonverbal feedback.

Empathy: Empathy is the ability to understand and share each other's feelings. In mindful communication, empathy helps build an emotional connection, allowing you to see situations from the other's perspective. This not only improves mutual understanding but also facilitates conflict resolution.

Clarity and Honesty: Expressing yourself clearly and honestly is crucial to avoid misunderstandings. Using direct and specific language, avoiding ambiguity, can help you communicate your thoughts and feelings more effectively. Being honest in your expressions promotes trust and transparency in relationships.

Non-judgment: Practicing a non-judgmental attitude means accepting the other person without criticism or blame. This approach fosters a safe communication environment, where both parties feel free to express themselves without fear of being judged.

Personal Responsibility: Taking responsibility for your emotions and reactions is essential in mindful communication. Using first-person phrases, such as "I feel" or "I think," rather than placing blame on others, can reduce conflict and promote more open and constructive communication.

Techniques to Improve Mindful Communication

Reflection: Repeat or paraphrase what the other person said to make sure you understood correctly. This shows care and can clear up any misunderstandings.

Open-Ended Questions: Ask open-ended questions that encourage the other person to express their thoughts and feelings in more detail. Avoid closed-ended questions that can be answered with a simple "yes" or "no."

Pause Time: Take short pauses during the conversation to reflect on what was said before responding. This can help you avoid knee-jerk reactions and respond in a more thoughtful manner.

Body Language Awareness: Being aware of your body language and facial expressions. These nonverbal cues can communicate a lot and affect the tone of the conversation.

Emotion Management: Recognizing and regulating your emotions during conversation. If you're feeling overwhelmed, it can be helpful to pause and return to the discussion when you're calmer.

Applications of Conscious Communication

Mindful communication can be applied in various contexts of daily life, improving personal and professional relationships:

Intimate Relationships: Improving communication with your partner can strengthen emotional bonding and resolve conflicts more effectively.

Work Environment: Fostering a culture of open and honest communication can improve collaboration and productivity.

Family: Using mindful communication techniques with family members can improve mutual understanding and reduce tensions.

Friendships: Being present and attentive in conversations with friends can strengthen relationships and create stronger emotional support.

Mindful communication is a critical skill for building meaningful relationships and dealing with conflict constructively. Through active listening, empathy, clarity, and honesty, we can improve our ability to communicate and connect with others. Practicing mindful communication requires commitment and ongoing awareness, but the benefits that come with it, both on a personal and relational level, are immeasurable.

6.1 Principles of Effective Communication

Effective communication is essential for building and maintaining healthy relationships, both personal and professional. It involves not only the ability to express oneself clearly, but also the ability to listen to and understand others. The principles of effective communication can be applied in various contexts to improve mutual understanding and reduce conflict.

Clarity and Precision

Being clear and precise in your communication is crucial. This means expressing your thoughts and feelings directly and specifically, avoiding ambiguities and generalizations. For example, instead of saying "you're always like this," it's more effective to say, "when you do this, I feel this way." Using concrete examples helps to make the message more understandable and less prone to misunderstanding.

Active Listening

Active listening is a key element of effective communication. It involves giving complete attention to the interlocutor, showing interest and understanding through verbal and nonverbal feedback. Active listening techniques include maintaining eye contact, nodding your head, and reflecting or paraphrasing what was said to make sure you understood correctly.

Empathy

Empathy is about putting yourself in the other person's shoes to understand their emotions and perspectives. This does not necessarily mean agreeing but showing respect and understanding for the feelings of others. Empathy facilitates more open and honest communication, creating an environment of trust and mutual respect.

Non-Judgment

Adopting a non-judgmental attitude means accepting the feelings and opinions of others without criticizing them. This attitude promotes a safe environment where people feel free to express themselves without fear of being judged. Reducing prejudice and keeping an open mind are essential components of this principle.

Constructive Feedback

Providing feedback constructively is essential for effective communication. Feedback should be specific, behaviour-oriented, and offered with the intent to improve, not criticize. Using the "sandwich method," starting with a positive comment, followed by constructive criticism, and ending with another positive comment, can be an effective way to communicate criticism constructively.

Non-verbal communication

Nonverbal communication, such as body language, facial expressions, and tone of voice, plays a crucial role in conveying the message. Being aware of your own body language and observing that of others can provide important insights into emotions and attitudes, complementing and reinforcing the verbal message.

Recognizing and Regulating Emotions

Emotions can significantly affect communication. Recognizing your emotions and learning to regulate them is key to communicating effectively. Emotion management techniques, such as mindfulness and deep breathing, can help maintain calm and clarity during difficult conversations.

Ask for clarification

Don't be afraid to ask for clarification if something isn't clear. Asking open ended questions can help you gain a deeper understanding of each other's message. This also shows interest and engagement in the conversation.

The principles of effective communication are powerful tools that can significantly improve the quality of interpersonal relationships. Being clear and precise, practicing active listening, showing empathy, avoiding judgment, providing constructive feedback, being aware of nonverbal communication, recognizing and regulating emotions, and asking for clarification are all essential elements for effective communication. Implementing these principles in daily life requires practice and awareness, but the benefits that come with them in terms of improving relationships and mutual understanding are invaluable.

6.2 Overcoming Barriers to Vulnerability

Vulnerability is an essential component of authentic and meaningful relationships, but many people find it difficult to embrace it due to emotional and psychological barriers. These barriers may stem from past experiences of rejection, fear of judgment, or lack of confidence in oneself and others. Overcoming these barriers is key to improving the quality of interpersonal relationships and developing more open and honest communication.

Recognizing Fears

The first step in overcoming barriers to vulnerability is to recognize the underlying fears. These may include:

Fear of Rejection: Fear of being rejected or not accepted can prevent you from being vulnerable. This fear often stems from past experiences of rejection or abandonment.

Fear of Judgment: Fear of being judged negatively by others can block your willingness to express authentic feelings and thoughts. This fear can be fuelled by excessive perfectionism or a critical self-image.

Fear of Showing Weaknesses: Many people see vulnerability as a weakness, believing that showing their emotions makes them less strong or capable. This can be especially true in cultural or family settings where independence and self-reliance are highly valued.

Building Self-Confidence

Building self-confidence is a crucial step in overcoming barriers to vulnerability. Here are some strategies:

Self-compassion: Treat yourself with the same kindness and understanding that you would offer to a friend. Recognize that everyone has imperfections and that it's normal to make mistakes.

Self-Acceptance: Learning to accept all parts of oneself, including weaknesses and imperfections. This process can be supported by mindfulness and meditation practices that promote self-acceptance.

Recognize Your Successes: Keeping a journal of your successes and positive experiences can help you build a more balanced and positive view of yourself.

Creating a Safe Environment

A secure environment is essential to facilitate vulnerability. This may include:

Trusting Relationships: Cultivating relationships with people who demonstrate empathy, understanding, and acceptance. These relationships can offer vital emotional support.

Open Communication: Promote open and honest communication where all parties feel free to express their thoughts and feelings without fear of judgment.

Sharing Spaces: Create spaces where vulnerability is encouraged and valued, such as support groups, group therapy, or circles of close friends.

Practicing Vulnerability

Vulnerability is a practice that takes time and effort. Here are some techniques to get you started:

Gradual Sharing: Start sharing small pieces of yourself with people you trust, gradually increasing the level of openness as trust grows.

Recognizing and Expressing Emotions: Learn to recognize your emotions and express them clearly and honestly. This can include using first-person phrases such as "I feel" to communicate how you feel without accusing others.

Empathic Listening: Practicing empathetic listening with others, showing that you are willing to understand and accept their vulnerabilities. This can create a mutual environment of trust and openness.

Benefits of the Vulnerability

Embracing vulnerability can lead to numerous benefits, including:

Deeper Relationships: Vulnerability allows you to create authentic and deep connections with others, based on mutual understanding and acceptance.

Greater Authenticity: Being vulnerable helps you live more authentically, allowing you to express your true nature without masks or defences.

Personal Growth: Vulnerability facilitates personal growth, allowing you to face your fears and develop greater emotional resilience.

Overcoming barriers to vulnerability is a process that requires courage and determination, but the benefits that come with it can significantly transform the quality of relationships and emotional well-being. Acknowledging one's fears, building self-confidence, creating a safe environment, and practicing vulnerability are key steps in opening up to others in an authentic and meaningful way. Embracing vulnerability not only improves interpersonal relationships but also fosters a fuller, more authentic life.

6.3 Tools to Improve Connection

Building authentic and deep connections in interpersonal relationships requires the use of various tools and techniques that promote mutual understanding, empathy, and effective communication. These tools can help overcome emotional barriers and create an environment where everyone feels understood and respected.

Reflective Listening

Reflective listening is a technique that involves not only actively listening to what the other person is saying but also reflecting back on what you've heard to make sure you've understood correctly. This method shows the interlocutor that you are paying attention and value their perspective.

Reflecting Feelings: After someone has spoken, repeat in your own words what you have understood, focusing on the emotions expressed. For example, "You seem to be frustrated because the project isn't progressing as planned."

Clarification: If something isn't clear, ask for more details. "Can you explain more about what you mean when you say you feel ignored?"

Nonviolent Communication (NVC)

Nonviolent Communication, developed by Marshall Rosenberg, is a process that helps to express one's needs clearly and respectfully, and to understand the needs of others. NVC is based on four components:

Observations: Describe hard facts without judgment or interpretation. "When I see that you don't respond to my messages..."

Feelings: Express how you feel about the observations. "... I feel worried and confused..."

Needs: Identify the underlying needs of feelings. "... Because I need clarity and connection."

Requests: Make a specific and achievable request. "Could you let me know if you'd prefer to communicate at another time?"

Assertiveness Techniques

Being assertive means expressing your thoughts and feelings clearly and directly, while also respecting the rights and feelings of others. Here are some techniques to improve assertiveness:

First-Person Messages: Use phrases that begin with "I" to express how you feel without accusing the other person. "I feel overwhelmed when work isn't distributed equally."

Body Language: Maintain open and positive body language, such as eye contact and a relaxed posture, to reinforce the verbal message.

Repetition: If your request is not initially complied with, repeat it calmly and firmly. "I understand you're busy, but it's important to me that this is resolved."

Gratitude Practice

Expressing gratitude is a powerful tool for strengthening relationships. Acknowledging and appreciating others for their positive actions and qualities can improve emotional connection.

Recognize Small Gestures: Express gratitude even for the little things the other person does. "Thank you for making dinner, I really appreciate it."

Gratitude journal: Keeping a journal in which you write down the things you are grateful for each day can help you maintain a positive outlook and express gratitude more easily.

Sharing Experiences and Interests

Sharing common experiences and interests can create fertile ground for connection. Participating together in activities that you both find enjoyable or meaningful can strengthen the bond.

Shared Activities: Plan activities that you both find enjoyable, such as excursions, hobbies, or cultural events.

Telling Stories: Sharing personal stories can help create a sense of closeness and understanding for each other.

Using specific tools and techniques to improve connection in relationships can lead to more authentic and meaningful interactions. Reflective listening, non-violent communication, assertiveness techniques, gratitude practice, and sharing experiences are all elements that can facilitate the building of deep and respectful bonds. Implementing these practices requires commitment and awareness, but the benefits in terms of relationship quality and emotional wellbeing are enormous.

Chapter 7: Rebuilding Trust

Rebuilding trust is an essential process for emotional well-being and the quality of interpersonal relationships. Trust, once broken, can be difficult to recover, but it's not impossible. With commitment, awareness and appropriate strategies, it is possible to regenerate this fundamental pillar of human relationships.

Understanding the Nature of Trust

Trust is the foundation of all healthy relationships. It's the assurance that the other person is trustworthy, honest, and cares about our well-being. When trust is compromised, a cycle of suspicion, anxieties, and insecurities sets in that can profoundly damage one's daily interactions and self-perception.

The Roots of Loss of Confidence

The causes of loss of trust are manifold and can include betrayal, lies, broken promises, infidelity, and lack of consistency in behaviour. These events leave emotional scars that take time and effort to heal. It is crucial to understand the source of the damage to be able to start a proper recovery process.

Strategy for Rebuilding Trust

Open and Honest Communication: Transparency is key. Openly expressing your feelings, admitting mistakes, and discussing concerns without accusing the other person can create an environment of mutual understanding.

Take Responsibility: Those who have broken trust must take full responsibility for their actions, without justification or minimization. This act of acknowledgment is a first step towards healing.

Repairing the Damage: Making amends is essential. This may include concrete actions that demonstrate a desire to undo the harm caused, such as changing behaviours or complying with new agreed rules.

Time and Patience: Trust cannot be rebuilt quickly. It takes time, during which both partners must be patient and understanding, recognizing that the healing process is gradual.

Building New Positive Experiences: Creating new memories and positive experiences can help replace negative ones. Doing activities together that strengthen connection, and shared joy can be very beneficial.

Professional Counselling: Sometimes, the support of a therapist can ease the process of rebuilding trust by offering tools and techniques to deal with difficulties more effectively.

Self-Healing Techniques

Mindfulness and Meditation: These practices can help you stay present and manage the anxiety and fear that often accompany loss of confidence.

Personal Journal: Writing down your thoughts and feelings can help you process your emotions and track your progress in the healing process.

Social Support: Having a support network made up of friends and family can provide comfort and advice during difficult times.

Self-confidence

Rebuilding trust in others is closely linked to self-confidence. Feeling confident in your abilities and worth is crucial to establishing and maintaining healthy relationships. Working on your self-esteem and recognizing your strengths can facilitate your ability to trust others.

Benefits of Rebuilt Trust

Once rebuilt, trust strengthens relationships, making them more resilient and authentic. People who can overcome the breakdown of trust often develop a deeper and more meaningful connection. Renewed trust leads to greater transparency, more open communication, and more effective cooperation.

Rebuilding trust is a challenging journey, but the benefits that come with it can profoundly transform relationships and quality of life. With patience, commitment, and the right strategies, it is possible to overcome the wounds of the past and create a future of understanding, respect, and authentic connection. Trust is the backbone of relationships, and once it's restored, it can make human connections stronger and longer lasting.

7.1 Facing and Overcoming the Wounds of the Past

Past wounds can have a lasting impact on our emotional well-being and ability to trust others. Overcoming these wounds requires awareness, commitment, and specific strategies to deal with and heal emotional scars. In this subchapter, we will explore the key steps to confront and overcome the wounds of the past.

Recognizing Emotional Wounds

The first step to overcoming the wounds of the past is to recognize them. Many people tend to ignore or downplay their painful emotions, hoping that they will disappear on their own. However, it is essential to admit the existence of these wounds and recognize their impact on one's life. This can include injuries related to betrayal, abandonment, criticism, or traumatic experiences.

Processing Emotions

Once the emotional wounds are recognized, the next step is to process the associated emotions. This can be done in different ways:

Individual Therapy: Working with a therapist can provide a safe and supportive environment to explore emotions and develop healing strategies.

Support Groups: Participating in support groups with people who have gone through similar experiences can offer comfort and mutual understanding.

Therapeutic Writing: Keeping a journal can help you express and understand your emotions. Writing about painful experiences can be a powerful way to process and release pain.

Self-compassion

Self-compassion is fundamental in the healing process. Treating yourself with kindness and understanding, rather than judgment and criticism, helps build a foundation of emotional security. This involves acknowledging that everyone makes mistakes and that the path to healing is unique to everyone.

Cognitive Restructuring

Cognitive restructuring is a useful technique for modifying negative and dysfunctional thoughts related to past wounds. This process includes:

Identifying Dysfunctional Thoughts: Recognizing negative automatic thoughts that arise in response to painful memories.

Replacing Negative Thoughts: Develop more balanced and positive alternative thoughts. For example, replace "I'll never be able to trust again" with "I can learn to trust gradually and cautiously."

Checking the Evidence: Examine the evidence supporting negative thoughts and challenge them with objective, realistic facts.

Healing Practices

Incorporating healing practices into daily life can support the process of overcoming past wounds:

Meditation and Mindfulness: These practices can help you stay present and manage difficult emotions without being overwhelmed.

Exercise: Physical activity can help reduce stress and improve emotional well-being. Even simple activities such as walking in the fresh air can have a positive effect.

Art and Creativity: Expressing one's emotions through art, music, dance, or other creative forms can be a powerful way to process and release grief.

Building Healthy Relationships

Part of the healing process includes building healthy and supportive relationships. This involves:

Setting Boundaries: Learn how to establish and maintain healthy boundaries in relationships to protect your emotional well-being.

Open Communication: Practicing open and honest communication with loved ones, expressing your own needs and listening to the needs of others.

Seek Support: Don't hesitate to seek support from friends, family, or professionals when needed. Having a support network can make a big difference in the healing process.

Overcoming the wounds of the past is a challenging but possible path. Acknowledging and processing emotions, practicing self-compassion, restructuring negative thoughts, and integrating healing practices into daily life are critical steps to emotional healing. With patience and determination, it is possible to let go of the pain of the past and build a more serene and fulfilling future.

7.2 Steps to Self-Confidence and Others: Building Confidence in Self and Others

Building confidence in yourself and others is a critical process for developing healthy and satisfying relationships. This path requires time, awareness, and consistent practice, but the benefits are invaluable. Here are some key steps to build confidence in yourself and others:

1. Self-Awareness and Self-Acceptance

1. Recognizing Your Strengths and Weaknesses:
2. The first stage of building self-confidence is to become aware of your abilities and areas for improvement. This can be done through personal reflection, feedback from others, and self-evaluation.
3. Practicing Self-Compassion:
4. Accepting yourself, including your flaws, is essential for developing solid confidence. Self-compassion involves treating yourself with the same kindness and understanding that you would treat a close friend. Instead of harshly criticizing yourself for mistakes, it's important to recognize them as opportunities for growth and learn from them.
5. Set Realistic Goals:
6. Setting achievable and measurable goals helps build trust. Every little success strengthens the perception of one's own abilities and motivates one to keep improving. It's crucial to celebrate progress, no matter how small it may seem.
7.

2. Trust in Others: Building Relationships Based on Trust

1. Be Reliable and Consistent:
2. Trust is built through reliability. Keeping promises and being consistent in behaviour helps establish a sense of security in relationships. When others can count on us, trust naturally grows.
3. Open and Honest Communication:
4. Transparent communication is the key to building trust. Being honest about your feelings, thoughts, and intentions creates an environment

of openness and understanding. In addition, listening actively and with empathy demonstrates respect and consideration for the other person.

1. Respect and Acceptance:
2. Accepting others for who they are and respecting their opinions and feelings helps build relationships based on trust. Avoiding negative judgments and criticism allows you to create a safe space where people feel valued and understood.

3. Facing and Overcoming Fears

1. Recognizing Fears:
2. Fear of rejection or failure can hinder trust-building. Identifying and acknowledging these fears is the first step to overcoming them. Often, these fears are rooted in past experiences that have left emotional scars.
3. Gradually Deal with Fear-Generating Situations:
4. Gradually exposing yourself to fear-generating situations helps you desensitize and build confidence. Starting with small steps, such as opening up more to a trusted friend, can progressively lead to greater confidence in social interactions.
5. Seek Support:
6. There is nothing wrong with seeking help when you face difficulties in building trust. Therapists, coaches, and support groups can offer tools and strategies to overcome fears and build confidence.

Building confidence in yourself and others is an ongoing journey that requires commitment and patience. Through self-awareness, self acceptance, trustworthiness, open communication, and facing fears, it is possible to create stronger and more meaningful relationships. Trust not only improves our relationships, but also our quality of life, making us more resilient and confident in the face of daily challenges.

7.3 Reconnecting with Intimacy

Reconnecting with intimacy is a critical step in rebuilding deep and meaningful relationships, especially after experiences that have compromised trust. Intimacy goes beyond simple physical contact, including emotional sharing and vulnerability. This process takes time, effort, and open communication.

Creating a Safe Environment

To reconnect with intimacy, it is essential to create a safe environment where both partners feel comfortable expressing their feelings without fear of judgment or rejection. This may include:

Listening Space: Establish moments dedicated to listening to each other, where each partner can express their thoughts and feelings freely.

Respect for Boundaries: Respect everyone's boundaries and don't force discussions or contacts that may make you uncomfortable.

Exploring the Vulnerability

Authentic intimacy requires vulnerability. Being open and honest about your fears, insecurities, and desires can strengthen the bond between your partners. Some ways to explore the vulnerability include:

Sharing Experiences: Sharing personal experiences that have had a significant impact, both positive and negative, can help create a deeper emotional connection.

Express Your Needs: Clearly communicate your emotional and physical needs, allowing your partner to better understand how to offer support.

Strengthening the Emotional Connection

Emotional intimacy is the foundation of a healthy relationship. To strengthen this connection, several practices can be adopted:

Empathic Dialogue: Use empathetic communication techniques to understand and validate your partner's feelings. This involves listening without interruption and responding with understanding and respect.

Shared Activities: Participate together in activities that you both find meaningful and enjoyable. These shared experiences can create positive memories and strengthen bonding.

Renewing Physical Intimacy

Physical intimacy is an important aspect of many relationships, but it can be influenced by past experiences of mistrust or trauma. To renew physical intimacy, it is useful to:

Take Things Slowly: Proceed slowly, respecting each person's rhythm and boundaries. This can include non-sexual affectionate gestures such as hugs and caresses.

Communicate During Physical Contact: Openly discuss preferences and comforts during physical intimacy, making sure both partners feel comfortable and respected.

Developing Trust

Trust is essential for intimacy. To build and build confidence:

Consistency and Trustworthiness: Demonstrate consistency in words and actions, keeping promises, and showing trustworthiness.

Honesty and Transparency: Being honest about your feelings and intentions, creating an environment of mutual transparency.

Couples Therapy

When intimacy challenges are particularly complex, couples therapy can provide a safe space to explore and resolve issues. A therapist can help develop new communication strategies and overcome emotional barriers.

Reconnecting with intimacy requires patience, commitment, and open communication. Creating a safe environment, exploring vulnerability, strengthening emotional connection, and renewing physical intimacy are essential steps in building deep and meaningful relationships. With the right approach and support, you can overcome challenges and enjoy a richer and more fulfilling relationship life.

Chapter 8: From Theory to Practice

Understanding the principles of attachment and relationships is only the first step towards self-improvement. True transformation happens when you apply this knowledge in your daily life. This chapter explores practical strategies for implementing change, setting realistic goals, and maintaining progress over time.

Implementing Change Strategies

Develop an Action Plan:

Goal Identification: Determine specific, measurable, and achievable goals. For example, improve communication with your partner or better manage your emotions.

Create Actionable Steps: Break down goals into smaller, more manageable steps. This makes the change less intimidating and easier to manage.

Set a Timeline: Set realistic deadlines for each phase of the plan. This helps to maintain motivation and track progress.

Practicing Mindfulness:

Daily Meditation: Taking a few minutes each day to meditate can improve mindfulness and stress management.

Mindfulness in Daily Activities: Integrating mindfulness into daily activities such as eating, walking, or working. This helps you stay present and reduce anxiety.

Emotional Regulation Techniques:

Deep Breathing: Use breathing techniques to calm the nervous system during times of stress.

Positive Self-Talk: Replace negative thoughts with positive, realistic affirmations.

Set Realistic Goals

Specific: Clearly define what you want to achieve.

Measurable: Establish criteria to measure progress

Achievable: Make sure your goals are realistic and achievable.

Relevant: Goals should be relevant and meaningful to your growth path.

Time frame: Set a deadline by which to meet your goals.

Monitoring and Evaluation:

Record Progress: Keep a journal or use apps to track your progress toward your goals.

Periodic Assessments: Regularly review goals and progress to make adjustments.

Overcoming Obstacles

Identify Barriers: Recognize potential difficulties that may prevent you from achieving your goals. This can include ingrained habits, lack of support, or excessive stress.

Coping Strategies: Develop strategies for dealing with and overcoming barriers. For example, seek social support, take small breaks to avoid burnout, or modify the environment to reduce temptations.

Resilience: Cultivating resilience to deal with setbacks. This includes learning from mistakes, maintaining a positive mindset, and adapting to changing circumstances.

Maintaining Change Over Time

Routines and Habits: Establish daily routines that support new behaviour's. Established habits make change sustainable in the long term.

Feedback & Support:

Support Groups: Participate in support groups or find a mentor who can offer guidance and encouragement.

Continuous Feedback: Ask for feedback from trusted people to continuously improve.

Self-Reflection:

Personal Journal: Keep a journal to reflect on progress, challenges, and lessons learned.

Review Sessions: Schedule regular sessions to review your goals and make necessary adjustments.

Celebrating Successes: Recognize and celebrate progress, even the smallest ones. This strengthens motivation and self-efficacy.

Moving from theory to practice requires commitment, perseverance, and careful planning. By implementing change strategies, setting realistic goals, overcoming obstacles, and maintaining change over time, you can transform your life in a meaningful way. The key to success lies in continuous awareness, flexibility and the ability to adapt to change. With the right approach, each individual can achieve lasting personal growth and healthier, more fulfilling relationships.

8.1 Daily Strategies for Change

Implementing day-to-day strategies for change is key to turning theory into practice. These practical approaches help to integrate new behaviour's and habits into everyday life, making the process of personal growth more manageable and sustainable.

Establish mindful routines.

1. Planning the Day:
2. Create a Schedule: Organize your day with specific activities and dedicated time for each task. This helps to maintain focus and reduce stress.
3. Time for Reflexivity: Set aside specific moments for reflection, planning, and evaluating progress.

Morning Routine:

1. Mindfulness on Awakening: Start your day with a few minutes of meditation or deep breathing to centre your mind.
2. Goals of the Day: Write down the main goals of the day, keeping them specific and achievable.

Evening Routine:

1. Evening Reflection: Take time to reflect on the day's successes and challenges. This helps you better prepare for the next day.
2. Relax and Decompression: Incorporate relaxing activities such as reading, hot bathing, or meditation to improve sleep quality.

Self-Care Habits

1. Balanced diet:
2. Nutritious Food: Supplement a balanced diet that supports physical and mental health.
3. Mindful Eating: Practicing mindful eating, paying attention to physical sensations and tastes during meals.

Regular exercise:

1. Daily Physical Activity: Exercise regularly, even with short sessions of activities such as walking, yoga, or stretching.
2. Body-Mind Connection: Choose activities that promote the connection between body and mind, such as tai chi or Pilates.

Quality Sleep:

1. Sleep Routine: Establish an evening routine that prepares your body and mind for sleep by reducing the use of electronic devices before bed.
2. Resting Environment: Create a comfortable sleeping environment, with adequate temperature and dimming of lights.

Stress Management

1. Relaxation Techniques:
2. Deep Breathing: Practice deep breathing exercises to calm the mind and reduce stress.
3. Guided Meditation: Use apps or recordings of guided meditations to help focus your mind.

Leisure Activities:

1. Hobbies and Interests: Making time for hobbies and activities that bring joy and satisfaction.
2. Time in Nature: Spending time outdoors can improve emotional wellbeing and reduce stress.

Time Management Tools

1. To-Do List:
2. Prioritization: Create to-do lists, sorting tasks by importance and urgency.
3. Division of Tasks: Break up larger tasks into smaller, more manageable steps.

Productivity Techniques:

Pomodoro Technique: Use the Pomodoro technique, working for 25 minutes followed by a short break, to keep productivity high.

Batching: Group similar tasks together to reduce transition time between tasks.

Support & Responsibility

1. Partner Responsibility:

2. Regular Check-In: Find a responsible partner with whom you can take stock of the situation regularly, sharing progress and challenges.
3. Constructive Feedback: Offer and receive constructive feedback to continuously improve.

Social Support:

1. Communities and Groups: Participate in support groups or online communities that share similar goals.
2. Family Involvement: Involve the family in their growth path to gain emotional and practical support.

Maintaining Motivation

1. Celebrating Successes:
2. Recognition of Progress: Celebrating progress, even small progress, to keep motivation high.
3. Personal Rewards: Establish small rewards for achieving specific goals.
4.

Vision Board:

Goal Visualization: Create a vision board with images and words that represent your goals and dreams. This visual tool can keep motivation high.

Adopting daily strategies for change helps to integrate new behaviours into everyday life, making personal growth sustainable and manageable. Establishing mindful routines, practicing self-care, managing stress, using time management tools, seeking support, and maintaining motivation are all crucial elements for long-term success. By implementing these strategies, you can turn theory into practice and achieve a more balanced and fulfilling life.

8.2 Setting Goals and Tracking Progress

Setting goals and tracking progress is essential to maintaining change over time. Careful planning and monitoring help you stay motivated, correct your route when necessary, and celebrate successes along the way.

Setting Clear and Realistic Goals

1. Specific: Goals should be well-defined and clear. For example, instead of saying "I want to be fitter," you can say "I want to exercise for 30 minutes, five days a week."
2. Measurable: They must include criteria that allow progress to be measured. For example, "lose 5 kg in three months".
3. Attainable: They need to be realistic, considering their own resources and limitations.
4. Relevant: Goals should be meaningful and aligned with your priorities and values.
5. Timing: They must have a clear deadline to maintain a sense of urgency and direction.
6.

Long-term vision:

1. Life Goals: Identify goals that reflect your long-term aspirations and visions, such as career growth, improved relationships, or physical health.
2. Split into Milestones: Divide long-term goals into short- and medium term goals to make them more manageable.

Plan and Implement

1. Detailed Planning:
2. Step by Step: Create a detailed plan that breaks down your goals into specific actions to be taken daily or weekly.

3. Resources Needed: Identify the resources needed, such as time, tools, or support, to achieve each step.

Systematic Implementation:

1. Routines: Integrate planned actions into daily and weekly routines.
2. Flexibility: Be prepared to adapt plans in response to obstacles or changes in circumstances.

Tracking Progress

1. Tracking Progress:
2. Logbook: Use a journal or app to record your daily activities and progress. Write down successes, challenges, and how they were overcome.
3. Charts and Tables: Create charts or tables to visualize your progress over time. This helps to maintain motivation and identify positive patterns or areas for improvement.

Periodic evaluations:

1. Self-Assessment: Schedule regular moments of self-assessment to reflect on progress and future steps. This can be done weekly, monthly, or quarterly.
1. External Feedback: Asking for feedback from people you trust, such as friends, family, or mentors, to get different perspectives on your progress.

Adapt and Correct

2. Flexibility and Adaptation:
3. Review Goals: Be prepared to review and adjust goals based on progress and circumstances. This may mean adjusting timing, changing priorities, or introducing new goals.

4. Alternative Strategies: If one approach doesn't work, explore alternative strategies and adjust your plan of action accordingly.

Overcoming Obstacles:

1. Identifying Barriers: Recognize the main obstacles that arise and develop strategies to overcome them. This can include time management, finding resources, or upskilling others.
2. Emotional Resilience: Cultivating resilience to cope with emotional challenges and maintain motivation. Practices such as mindfulness and self-compassion can be particularly helpful.

Celebrating Successes

1. Recognize Milestones:

2. Small Successes: Celebrating even small milestones keeps motivation high. This can include symbolic rewards or moments of positive reflection.
3. Great Successes: When you achieve significant goals, take the time to celebrate properly, perhaps sharing the success with friends and family.

Gratitude:

1. Gratitude journal: Keeping a journal where you write down the things you're grateful for can help you maintain a positive mindset and recognize the progress you've made.
2. Positive Reflections: Take time to reflect on the progress you have made and the path you have taken, acknowledging your commitment and determination.

Setting clear goals and tracking progress are key to long-term success. With a detailed action plan, a well-defined routine, and tools to track and adapt your journey, you can turn your ambitions into reality. By celebrating successes and maintaining a flexible and resilient mindset, each individual can achieve meaningful and lasting personal growth

8.3 Maintaining Change Over Time

Maintaining change is an essential component of the personal growth journey. Once you've implemented new habits and strategies, it's important to make sure they become an integral part of your daily life. Maintaining change requires commitment, perseverance, and a series of specific techniques to avoid falling back into old patterns.

Consolidating New Habits

1. Stable Routine:
2. Consistency: Maintain a daily and weekly routine that includes new habits. Consistency helps to entrench these changes in everyday life.
3. Simplicity: Start with small, easy-to-manage changes and gradually add new habits. Simplicity helps avoid overload and makes continuity more likely.

Positive Reinforcements:

1. Rewards: Reward yourself for maintaining new habits. Rewards can be as simple as a moment of relaxation or an enjoyable activity.
2. Self-reinforcing: Recognize and celebrate your successes internally. Express self-appreciation for one's commitment and determination.

Continuous monitoring

1. Tracking Tools:
2. App Tracking: Use apps to track your progress and habits. These apps can provide reminders and progress views.
3. Journal: Continue to keep a journal to record your progress, challenges, and reflections. This helps to maintain awareness and identify any areas for improvement.

Periodic evaluations:

1. Monthly Check-ins: Schedule monthly check-ins to assess progress against your initial goals. This allows you to make adjustments and stay motivated.
2. Third-Party Feedback: Seek feedback from people you trust to get different perspectives on your progress.

Adaptation and Flexibility

1. Coping with Relapse:
2. Accept Relapse: Understand that relapses are a natural part of the change process. Instead of getting discouraged, use relapses as opportunities to learn and improve.
3. Recovery Plan: Have a plan to recover quickly from relapses. This can include getting back into new habits right away and asking for support when needed.

Flexibility:

1. Adapt Goals: Be prepared to adjust goals and strategies based on changes in circumstances or new information.
2. Growth Mindset: Cultivating a growth mindset, which values continuous learning and adaptation. This helps to maintain a positive outlook even in the face of challenges.

Long-term support

1. Support Community:
2. Support Groups: Participate in support groups or communities that share similar goals. These groups can offer encouragement, accountability, and inspiration.
3. Mentors and Coaches: Having a mentor or coach can provide guidance, feedback, and ongoing support.

Social Networks:

1. Engage Friends and Family: Share your goals and progress with friends and family. Their support can be crucial in maintaining motivation.
2. Shared Activities: Participate in activities that support new goals with other people. This can make the process more enjoyable and sustainable. **Mindset and Motivation**

1. Positive Mindset:
2. Positive Thinking: Maintain a positive mindset, focusing on the progress made rather than the difficulties encountered.
3. Gratitude: Practice gratitude for small daily victories. This can increase motivation and overall well-being.

Visualization and Intentionality:

1. Visualize Success: Use visualization techniques to envision the achievement of goals. This strengthens determination and self-confidence.
2. Daily Intentionality: Start each day with a clear and focused intention. This helps to maintain direction and focus efforts on goals.

Maintaining change over time requires a combination of consistency, continuous monitoring, adaptability, and support. Consolidating new habits, monitoring progress, being flexible, and seeking support are key strategies to ensure change becomes permanent. With consistent commitment and a positive mindset, you can maintain progress and continue to grow personally, creating a more balanced and fulfilling life.

Chapter 9: Personal Action Plan

A personal action plan is an essential tool for turning goals and aspirations into tangible results. In this chapter, we'll explore how to create a detailed plan that will help you achieve your goals, overcome challenges, and stay motivated along the way.

Defining a Clear Vision

Dreams and Aspirations: Start by identifying your long-term dreams and aspirations. Think about what you really want to achieve in life, both personally and professionally. This vision will serve as a guide for your plan of action.

SMART Goals: Turn your vision into SMART (Specific, Measurable, Relevant, Time-Bound) goals. For example, if your dream is to improve your health, a SMART goal might be "lose 5 kg within three months through a balanced diet and regular exercise."

Planning Actions

Detail Actions: Break down each goal into specific, concrete actions. If your goal was to improve your professional skills, you could identify actions such as enrolling in an online course, reading a book a month about your field, and attending conferences.

Resources Needed: Identify the resources you need for each action, such as time, money, expertise, and external support. Plan how to get these resources to avoid any unforeseen events along the way.

Timeline and Deadlines: Assign specific deadlines for each action. Creating a timeline will help you stay focused and track your progress over time.

Implement and Monitor

Daily Routine: Integrate planned actions into your daily routine. Consistency is the key to turning temporary behaviours into long-lasting habits.

Tracking and Feedback: Use tracking tools like apps, journals, or spreadsheets to record your progress. Seek feedback from trusted mentors or friends to get an outside perspective on your progress.

Adapt and Improve

Flexibility: Be prepared to deal with obstacles and adjust your plan of action if necessary. Having a flexible approach will allow you to better respond to the challenges and opportunities that arise.

Continuous Learning: Learn from your successes and failures. Every experience, positive or negative, offers an opportunity for growth and improvement.

Maintaining Motivation

Celebrate Successes: Recognize and celebrate your successes, big and small. This strengthens your motivation and gives you the energy to keep going.

Rewards: Setting rewards for achieving goals helps you stay motivated. The rewards can be as simple as a day of relaxation or as meaningful as a trip.

Ongoing Support: Surround yourself with people who support and encourage you. Participate in support groups, seek out mentors, and share your progress with friends and family.

Creating and following a well-structured personal action plan is crucial to making your dreams a reality. Defining a clear vision, planning detailed actions, monitoring progress, adapting to circumstances, and maintaining motivation are the key steps to achieving success. With commitment and perseverance, you can achieve your goals and live a more satisfying and fulfilled life.

9.1 Developing Your Action Plan

Creating a personalized action plan is essential to translate intentions into concrete results. Here's a step-by-step guide to developing an effective action plan that will help you achieve your goals and overcome challenges.

Step 1: Set clear goals.

Identify Areas for Improvement: Reflect on the various aspects of your life that you want to improve, such as your career, health, relationships, or personal development. Make a list of these areas.

Establish SMART Goals: For each area identified, define Specific, Measurable, (Achievable), Relevant, and Time-bound goals. For example, if you want to improve your health, a SMART goal might be "run 5K three times a week within three months."

Step 2: Asset Analysis

Resources Needed: Identify the resources needed to achieve your goals, such as time, money, tools, or skills. For example, if your goal is to improve your professional skills, you may need training courses or educational materials.

External Support: Consider the support you may need from friends, family, mentors, or coaches. These individuals can offer encouragement, advice, and feedback along the way.

Step 3: Plan Actions

Specific Actions: Break down each goal into specific, concrete actions. For example, if your goal is to run 5K three times a week, actions might include buying running shoes, finding running routes, and planning days and times to run.

Timeline: Establish a timeline for each action, with specific deadlines. For example, "Buy running shoes within the next week" or "Complete the first 5K within a month."

Step 4: Implementation

Daily Routine: Integrate planned actions into your daily routine. Consistency is crucial for developing new habits and maintaining discipline.

Tracking and Feedback: Use tracking tools like apps, journals, or spreadsheets to record your progress. Seek feedback from trusted mentors or friends to get an outside perspective on your progress.

Step 5: Adapt and Improve

Flexibility: Be prepared to deal with obstacles and adjust your plan of action if necessary. Having a flexible approach will allow you to better respond to the challenges and opportunities that arise.

Continuous Learning: Learn from your successes and failures. Every experience, positive or negative, offers an opportunity for growth and improvement.

Step 6: Stay Motivated

Celebrate Successes: Recognize and celebrate your successes, big and small. This strengthens your motivation and gives you the energy to keep going.

Rewards: Setting rewards for achieving goals helps you stay motivated. The rewards can be as simple as a day of relaxation or as meaningful as a trip.

Ongoing Support: Surround yourself with people who support and encourage you. Participate in support groups, seek out mentors, and share your progress with friends and family.

Sample Action Plan

Actions:

1. Purchase running clothing and shoes within a week.
2. Find three running routes near your home within two weeks.
3. Schedule running sessions for Monday, Wednesday, and Friday at 7:00 a.m.
4. Sign up for a local 5K race within a month.

Resources:

1. Budget for running clothing.
2. Local maps or running route apps.
3. Support from a friend or a running group.

Timeline:

1. Actions to be completed within the next two weeks.
2. Weekly progress review.
3. Aim to run 5 km for three months.

A well-structured personal action plan is essential to turn aspirations into reality. Defining a clear vision, planning detailed actions, monitoring progress, adapting to circumstances, and maintaining motivation are the key steps to achieving success. With commitment and perseverance, you can achieve your goals and live a more satisfying and fulfilled life.

9.2 Setting Short-Term and Long-Term Goals

Being able to maintain a steady path towards your goals requires the ability to distinguish between what you want to achieve in the short term and what you want to accomplish in the long run. This chapter will explore how to set effective goals and maintain motivation to achieve them.

Setting short-term goals

1. Specificity: They must be clear and well-defined. For example, "Read one book a month."
2. Measurability: They must be easily monitored. Use specific metrics or milestones.
3. Tight timeline: They need to have tight deadlines, such as weeks or a few months.

Examples of Short-Term Goals:

1. Health: Go to the gym three times a week.
2. Career: Complete an online course in two months.
3. Relationships: Plan a special evening with your partner every two weeks.

Setting long-term goals

1. Broad Vision: They must reflect larger, long-term aspirations.
2. Continuous Commitment: They require constant and prolonged commitment.
3. Flexibility: They need to be flexible enough to adapt to changes over time.

Examples of Long-Term Goals:

1. Health: Run a marathon within a year.
2. Career: Advance in the role or get a promotion within three years.
3. Relationships: Build a deeper, more meaningful relationship with your partner through shared activities and open communication.

Connecting Short-Term and Long-Term Goals

1. Alignment: Make sure your short-term goals align with your long-term goals. Every small step should help achieve the bigger picture.

2. Gradual Progression: Use short-term goals as milestones that progressively bring you closer to long-term goals.
3. Periodic Assessments: Review your goals regularly to make sure you're on the right track. Adjust your short-term goals as necessary to stay aligned with long-term ones.

Monitoring and Adjusting Goals

1. Apps & Software: Use time and task management apps to track progress.
2. Journals and Planners: Writing down your goals and progress in a journal can provide a tangible insight into your efforts.

Flexibility and Adaptation:

1. Recognize Challenges: Be aware of difficulties that may arise and be prepared to change them.
2. Continuous Feedback: Ask for regular feedback and make adjustments as necessary to stay on track with your goals.

Maintaining Motivation

1. Rewards: Establish rewards for reaching milestones. This keeps your spirits up and motivates you to keep going.
2. Social Support: Share your goals with friends, family, or support groups for encouragement.
3. Self-Reflection: Take time to reflect on the progress you've made and celebrate successes, even small ones.

Setting short- and long-term goals is key to maintaining direction and motivation on your path to personal growth. Linking these goals strategically, tracking progress, and adapting to circumstances are key steps in ensuring success. With determination and a well-structured plan, it is possible to turn aspirations into tangible and lasting realities.

9.3 Resources and Tools for Success

Achieving goals requires not only determination and a well-structured action plan, but also the use of appropriate resources and tools. This chapter explores several resources and tools that can ease the path to success.

Planning & Monitoring Tools

1. Taoist: A task management app that helps you organize your to-do lists, set deadlines, and track your progress.
2. Trello: A visual project management platform that uses boards and boards to keep track of tasks and projects.

Diari e Planner:

1. Bullet Journal: A customizable organization system that allows you to combine to-do lists, journals, calendars, and notes into a single notebook.
2. Weekly Planners: Use weekly planners to plan and view your tasks and goals for the week.

Educational Resources

1. "Atomic Habits" by James Clear: A book that explores how to build good habits and get rid of bad ones through small, daily changes.
2. "Mindset" by Carol S. Dweck: A work that explains the importance of the growth mindset and how to develop it to achieve success.

Online Courses:

1. Coursera and edX: Platforms that offer online courses on a wide range of topics, taught by prestigious universities and institutions.
2. Skill share: An online learning community with thousands of classes on creative, professional, and personal development topics.

Professional Support

1. Life Coach: A life coach can help you identify your goals, develop strategies for achieving them, and keep you motivated along the way.

2. Career Coach: A career coach can offer career development guidance and support, helping you make informed career choices and achieve your career goals.

Therapy:

1. Psychotherapy: A therapist can help you explore and address emotional blocks, past trauma, and mental health issues that can hinder your progress.
2. Cognitive-Behavioural Therapy (CBT): This form of therapy is particularly helpful in identifying and modifying negative thoughts and behaviour's.

Motivation and Self-Reflection Tools

1. Sciatica: Turn your goals and habits into a role-playing game, where you earn points and rewards by completing tasks.
2. Strider: A goal tracking app that helps you track progress and stay motivated.

Self-Reflection Techniques:

1. Meditation and Mindfulness: Daily meditation and mindfulness practices can help you stay present and manage stress.
2. Gratitude journal: Keeping a gratitude journal to reflect on what you are grateful for can increase your well-being and motivation.

Community and Support Networks

1. Meetup: A platform for finding and creating local groups based on common interests, including personal and professional growth goals.
2. Groups on Facebook: There are many groups on Facebook dedicated to various aspects of personal growth, where you can share experiences and receive support.

Professional Networks:

1. LinkedIn: Use LinkedIn to build a professional network, find mentors, and receive career development advice.
2. Professional Associations: Join professional associations to stay up to date on industry trends, attend conferences, and access exclusive resources.

The use of appropriate resources and tools is essential to support one's personal and professional growth. Time management apps, journals, online courses, professional support, self-reflection techniques, and supportive communities offer a solid foundation for achieving and maintaining your goals. With the right resources and a well-structured plan, you can overcome challenges and realize your full potential.

Chapter 10: Towards a Future of Growth and Sustainability

Closing this path of personal and relational growth requires the integration of the principles explored in the previous chapters. We learned about the importance of attachment, trust, mindful communication, and mindfulness practices. Now, we look forward to ensuring that these teachings become an integral part of our daily lives, allowing us to live sustainably and fulfilling. This chapter will focus on three key aspects: finding and cultivating purpose in life, sustainable management of personal energy, and continuous commitment to learning and adaptation.

Finding and Cultivating a Purpose in Life

Having a clear purpose in life is a powerful driver of motivation and satisfaction. It provides direction and meaning, allowing us to navigate through challenges with greater resilience.

Personal Reflection:

Finding your purpose starts with deep personal reflection. Ask yourself what you're passionate about, what your core values are, and how you wish to influence the world. Journaling can help you clarify your thoughts and define a more precise vision of your purpose.

Goal Alignment:

Once you've identified a purpose, it's essential to align your short- and long term goals with it. This ensures that your daily actions are consistent with your values and aspirations, keeping motivation high and ensuring continued progress.

Contribution to the Community:

Actively participating in the community can strengthen your sense of purpose. Volunteering, participating in local projects, or supporting causes you care about not only enriches your life but also creates a positive impact on the world around you.

Sustainable Personal Energy Management

Personal energy management is crucial for maintaining a work-life balance, preventing burnout, and ensuring overall well-being.

Daily Practices for Physical Health:

A balanced diet and regular physical activity are key. Be sure to include a variety of nutritious foods in your diet and make time for exercise, whether it's a run, yoga, or a walk.

Sleep and Rest:

Quality sleep is vital to recharge your batteries. Establish an evening routine that promotes relaxation and thus improves the quality of your sleep. Taking regular breaks throughout the workday helps maintain productivity and focus.

Stress Management Techniques:

Techniques such as deep breathing, mindfulness, and meditation are effective tools for managing stress. By integrating mindfulness into your daily routine, you can keep your mind present and reduce anxiety.

Continuous Commitment to Learning and Adaptation

In an ever-changing world, continuous learning and the ability to adapt to change are essential for lasting personal growth.

Growth Mindset:

Adopting a growth mindset means recognizing that skills and competencies can be developed through commitment and dedication. This positive attitude allows you to face challenges as opportunities for growth.

Continuing education:

Attending continuing education courses, reading books, and attending seminars helps you keep your skills up-to-date and gain new knowledge. Online platforms that offer a wide range of courses that you can take at your own pace.

Flexibility and Resilience:

The ability to adapt to change is critical for long-term success. Being flexible and resilient allows you to face difficulties with a positive and proactive mindset, turning obstacles into opportunities for growth.

Incorporating these three pillars – finding and cultivating purpose in life, sustainable management of personal energy, and continuous commitment to learning and adaptation – is essential to ensuring that personal growth and well-being last. Not only will these principles help you maintain emotional, mental, and physical balance, but they will also allow you to live a more fulfilling and fulfilled life. With constant commitment and a clear vision, it is possible to overcome challenges and build a future of continuous growth and lasting well-being.

10.1 Finding and Cultivating Purpose in Life

Having a clear and defined purpose in life is essential for maintaining motivation and well-being in the long run. It provides direction, meaning, and a source of positive energy that helps you overcome daily challenges. Finding one's purpose requires deep reflection; while cultivating it involves a constant effort to align one's actions and goals with this purpose.

Identifying Your Purpose

Personal Reflection:

1. The first step to finding your purpose is personal reflection. This process takes time and introspection. It's helpful to ask yourself questions like, "What am I really passionate about?", "What are my core values?", "What impact do I want to have on the world?". Taking the time to answer these questions can help clarify what's important to you.

Reflective Writing:

2. Keeping a journal can be an effective tool for exploring your thoughts and feelings. Writing regularly about your experiences, desires, and aspirations can help you identify recurring themes and form a clearer vision of your purpose. Reflective writing allows you to write down ideas that might be vague or confusing, making them more tangible and understandable.

Long-term vision:

3. Once you've identified a purpose, it's helpful to visualize how it will translate into concrete actions in the long run. Imagining where you would like to be in five or ten years can provide a mind map that guides your daily decisions and life choices. A long-term vision helps you stay motivated, especially when facing obstacles and challenges.

Goal Alignment

Short-Term and Long-Term Goals:

1. Setting goals that align with your purpose is crucial. Short-term goals help you take small, daily steps toward your vision, while long-term

goals keep you focused on the big picture. Make sure each goal is Specific, Measurable, Achievable, Relevant, and Timed (SMART).

Daily Actions:

2. Each day presents opportunities to make progress toward one's purpose. Incorporating daily actions that reflect your values and goals can help maintain consistency and strengthen your commitment. Even

    small steps, such as dedicating some time each day to a meaningful project or cause that is close to your heart, can make a big difference in the long run.

Monitoring and Adaptation:

3. Tracking progress is essential to staying on track. Using tools like journals, goal management apps, or planners can help you track progress and adjust when necessary. Being flexible and ready to adapt to changes and unforeseen events is just as important to maintain your path to your goal.

4.

Contribution to the Community

Active Participation:

1. Actively participating in the community can give you a deeper sense of purpose and belonging. Volunteering, participating in local projects, or supporting causes you care about not only enriches your life but also creates a positive impact on the world around you. Being a part of something bigger than ourselves helps us see the value of our daily actions and feel connected to others.

Significant Relationships:

2. Cultivating meaningful relationships is another way to live out your purpose. Sharing experiences and goals with friends, family, and colleagues creates a support network that can support you through

difficult times and celebrate your successes. Authentic and deeply connected relationships amplify the sense of accomplishment and satisfaction.

Group Initiatives:

3. Participating or initiating group initiatives can multiply the impact of your purpose. Whether it's organizing a charity event, forming a support group, or starting a community project, working together with others to achieve a common goal can be extremely rewarding. These collective experiences reinforce the sense of community and the belief that great things can be achieved together.

Finding and cultivating purpose in life is a continuous journey of reflection, action, and adaptation. This purpose provides clear direction, nurtures motivation, and strengthens a sense of accomplishment. By aligning personal goals with this purpose and actively contributing to the community, you can live a more meaningful and fulfilling life. Incorporating these practices into your daily routine not only ensures personal well-being but also creates a lasting positive impact in the world around you.

10.2 Sustainable Personal Energy Management

Managing personal energy sustainably is essential for maintaining a balance between different areas of life, preventing burnout, and ensuring overall wellbeing. This section explores the practices and strategies needed to maintain and optimize one's physical, mental, and emotional energy.

Daily Practices for Physical Health

Balanced diet:

1. A balanced diet is crucial for supporting the body and mind. Consuming a variety of nutritious foods, including fruits, vegetables, lean proteins, and whole grains, provides the energy you need to get through the day. It's important to avoid highly processed foods and refined sugars, which can cause energy spikes and dips.

Regular physical activity:

2. Physical activity not only improves physical health but also has positive effects on mental well-being. Cardiovascular exercises such as running, swimming, or cycling help keep the heart healthy and reduce stress. Strength and flexibility exercises, such as yoga and Pilates, improve muscle endurance and joint mobility, contributing to better posture and a reduced risk of injury.

Exercise Routine:

3. Incorporating exercise into your daily routine is essential for maintaining a consistent energy level. Starting your day with a short session of stretching or yoga exercises can help energize your body and mind. Similarly, ending the day with relaxing activities such as an evening walk can promote relaxation and improve sleep quality.

Sleep and Rest

Importance of Sleep:

1. Quality sleep is crucial for physical and mental recovery. Lack of sleep can lead to reduced cognitive function, increased stress, and long-term health problems. It's crucial to establish an evening routine that promotes relaxation and sleep preparation.

Creating a Resting Environment:

2. Make sure your sleeping environment is comfortable and free of distractions. Keeping the bedroom dark, quiet, and at a pleasant temperature helps improve sleep quality. Reducing exposure to bright

screens at least an hour before bed can prevent interference with natural sleep cycles.

Breaks during the Day:

3. In addition to a good night's sleep, it's important to take regular breaks throughout the workday to recharge. Short breaks of 5-10 minutes every hour can improve concentration and reduce fatigue. During

these breaks, practicing relaxation techniques such as deep breathing or short stretching exercises can be very helpful. **Stress Management Techniques**

Mindfulness and Meditation:

1. Mindfulness and meditation are effective tools for managing stress and maintaining emotional balance. Practicing mindfulness means being fully present in the moment, observing thoughts and feelings without judgment. Regular meditation helps calm the mind, reduce anxiety, and improve the ability to concentrate.

Breathing Exercises:

2. Breathing techniques, such as deep breathing and diaphragmatic breathing, can be used to reduce stress immediately. Practicing deep breathing for a few minutes can help calm the nervous system and bring the mind back to a state of tranquillity.

Relaxing Activities:

3. Incorporating relaxing activities into your daily routine can contribute significantly to stress management. Activities such as gardening, reading, art, or listening to music can offer a pleasant detachment from everyday worries and provide a sense of calm and satisfaction.

Managing personal energy sustainably is essential for maintaining a work-life balance, preventing burnout, and ensuring overall well-being. Through daily practices of balanced nutrition, regular physical activity, quality sleep, and stress management techniques, you can optimize your energy resources and live a more balanced and fulfilling life. Incorporating these strategies into your daily life will help maintain your physical, mental, and emotional health, allowing you to face challenges with greater resilience and positivity.

10.3 Continuous Commitment to Learning and Adaptation

In an ever-changing world, continuous learning and the ability to adapt to change are crucial for long-lasting and sustainable personal growth. This commitment allows you to face new challenges, seize opportunities and remain competitive in the professional field.

Growth Mindset

Developing a Growth Mindset:

1. Adopting a growth mindset means recognizing that skills and intelligences can be developed through commitment and dedication. This positive attitude allows you to see challenges as learning opportunities rather than insurmountable obstacles.

Accepting Errors as Part of the Process:

2. A growth mindset also involves accepting mistakes as a natural part of the learning journey. Mistakes offer valuable lessons that can guide you towards continuous improvement and innovation. Being open to constructive feedback and reflecting on past experiences is key to growth.

Learning from Success Models:

Observing and learning from those who have already achieved success in their field can be a source of inspiration and guidance. Studying the strategies and habits of successful people can provide practical guidance on how to improve one's skills and approaches.

Continuing education

Training Courses and Certifications:

1. Investing in continuing education and obtaining certifications can expand one's skills and open up new professional opportunities.

    Platforms that offer a wide range of courses on topics ranging from technical skills to soft skills.

Participation in Seminars and Workshops:

2. Attending seminars, workshops and conferences allows you to delve into specific areas of interest, exchange ideas with experts in the field and create networks of professional contacts. These events provide an opportunity to catch up on the latest trends and innovations.

Reading and Self-Directed Study:

3. Maintaining the habit of reading books, articles and specialized magazines is an effective way to enrich your knowledge. Choosing topics that stimulate curiosity, and personal passion makes learning an enjoyable and motivating activity. **Flexibility and Resilience**

Adapting to Change:

1. The ability to adapt quickly to change is a critical skill in a dynamic world. This requires an open mindset and a willingness to review and modify your plans and strategies in response to new information and circumstances.

Building Resilience:

2. Resilience is the ability to recover quickly from hardship. Cultivating resilience involves learning to manage stress, maintain a positive outlook, and use challenges as opportunities for growth. Practices such as mindfulness and meditation can help develop this important skill.

Innovation and Creativity:

1. Being innovative and creative is essential to staying relevant and competitive. This means not being afraid to experiment with new ideas and approaches, even if it comes with the risk of failure. Creativity can be stimulated through artistic activities, brainstorming, and collaborations with people from different disciplines.

Engaging in continuous learning and developing the ability to adapt to change are crucial elements for sustainable personal and professional growth. Adopting a growth mindset, investing in lifelong learning, and cultivating flexibility and resilience allow you to face challenges with confidence and seize new opportunities. Integrating these practices into your daily life will ensure not only long-term success but also a life full of meaning and satisfaction.

Conclusion

The application of the principles explored in this book creates the fertile ground for lasting personal and relational growth. Support for individual aspirations, aligned goals, and shared values creates a framework for a life that is not only surviving, but thriving. In this fabric of love, woven with transparency, honesty, and mutual respect, one discovers not only a union of hearts, but a sanctuary for trust, communication, and lasting companionship. Through the application of these values, you have transformed your life and relationships. You've learned how to manage stress, practice mindfulness, and build relationships based on trust and respect. These changes are not just choices, but investments in longevity and the depth of connections that transcend the ordinary, creating a tapestry of shared memories and a legacy of love.

By embracing respect as a guiding principle, you have strengthened the bridges between yourself and others, creating an environment where differences are celebrated, boundaries respected, and the intrinsic value of each person recognized. In a world that often rushes ahead, the timeless virtue of respect invites us to stop, listen, and appreciate the different narratives that form the human experience. May your interactions be imbued with the spirit of respect, creating a legacy of understanding, kindness, and lasting connections that stand the test of time. In the final pages of this book, you find not only a collection of exercises and reflections, but a map for a transformative connection. This book, a companion on the journey of personal growth, testifies to the belief that love is not a static entity but a dynamic, evolutionary force that can be nurtured and strengthened through intentional effort. As you engage with the exercises and reflections contained in these pages, embark on a shared exploration of emotions, communication patterns, and aspirations. This book becomes a bridge, facilitating conversations that may have gone unexpressed, offering tools to navigate the complexities of life. It is a guide through the labyrinth of emotions, gently illuminating the path to understanding, empathy, and growth. This book is not just a tool; It is an invitation to embark on a journey of self-discovery and relational enrichment, a testament to the enduring potential of love when nurtured with care and commitment.

BONUS

And now, you can access your exclusive bonus. Just get your mobile phone camera ready and scan the QR code below to enjoy it.

www.ingramcontent.com/pod-product-compliance
Lightning Source LLC
Chambersburg PA
CBHW060343170426
43202CB00014B/2861